NEW Z

Dan Colwell

JPMGUIDES

symbols from nature

CONTENTS

proud traditions

ocean splendours

scenic roads

THIS WAY NEW ZEALAND

The exhilarating beauty of New Zealand has been appreciated ever since the first explorer, said to be a Polynesian named Kupe, took home a story of a land of mountains shrouded in mist. His tale inspired others to settle there, and the subsequent Maori inhabitants called the country Aotearoa, or "land of the long white cloud".

Today, the country's many visitors still remark on the stunning scenery and the freshness and purity of the air—a luxury that the 4.4 million easy-going but hard-working inhabitants make the most of whenever they can: playing rugby and cricket in the towns, or hiking, swimming and mountaineering in the great outdoors.

A Little Geography

The archipelago that makes up New Zealand—the North Island, the South Island and a scattering of smaller islets—lies 2,250 km (1,400 miles) southeast of Australia and has a combined area of 270,534 sq km (104,453 sq miles), which makes it a little larger than Great Britain or about two-thirds of the size of California. Organizing your trip is relatively easy, given that both islands are served by good roads and excellent public transport systems. In fact, the only difficult thing is in knowing where to start, as they both have an abundance of areas of extraordinary natural beauty and fascinating manmade sights. The North Island is the warmest, with a subtropical region in the northernmost peninsula, while snow falls on the mountains of the South Island in the antipodean winter (June to September). Wind and rain are common occurrences in what is still quite an untamed land.

The capital, Wellington, is located at the southern tip of the North Island. The greatest competitor of this port and commercial centre is the faster-growing, more industrial city of Auckland to the north. These two cities perpetuate an old, good-humoured rivalry, for Wellington replaced Auckland as capital in 1865. The South Island is larger than the more developed North Island. With a million inhabitants, a third of them living in its main city of Christchurch, it is spacious enough to inspire escapists, adventurers and tourists who are simply seeking solitude and unforgettable natural beauty. The South Island also offers endless amounts of that delicious, clean air. From Stewart Island—New Zealand's third-largest—at its tip, you can sometimes see the ethereal lights of the *aurora australis* staining the southern sky.

Fauna
The shy kiwi, the national emblem, and the tuatara reptile, a relic from the dinosaur era, are rarely seen outside zoos. By far, the most numerous four-legged creatures are cattle and sheep, which were introduced by European settlers. After lambing in October, the sheep population outnumbers the human one by fourteen to one. On the shores of South Island you'll encounter seals and sea lions. Sperm whale live off the coast of Kaikoura and there are many seabirds.

Maori and Pakeha
Citizens of modern New Zealand hail from many parts of the world: in recent years there has been a substantial influx of people from Southeast Asia, while Auckland alone can boast a larger

Go underground. See beautiful stalactite and stalagmite sculptures and a cave lit by glow-worms at the remarkable **Waitomo Caves** on North Island.

population of Pacific islanders than any of the island nations of the Pacific. But the two most prominent groups are the original Maori peoples and the descendants of the European—mainly British—settlers. Their relationship, once uneasy, at times openly hostile and bloody, shaped the New Zealand of today.

When the first Europeans—called *pakeha*, or outsiders, by the Maori—arrived in the late 18th century, the native Maori population was at least 100,000; by the start of the 20th century that figure had dropped to 42,000. The main causes were the Maori's lack of resistance to European diseases and the effects of warfare, often between Maori tribes but also in the so-called New Zealand Wars, when the British colonial government and private companies seized Maori lands. The Maori population has seen a resurgence in recent years and now stands at more than 673,000, or 15 per cent of the total population.

Nonetheless, the vast majority of people in New Zealand today

—around 70 per cent—are of European extract. They have forged an independent identity based upon their island nation's geographical isolation and the recognition that they inhabit a Pacific country, not a European one. Admittedly, in recent years they have had to face up to the historical implications of that 19th-century land grab, as Maori tribes have won the legal right to reclaim territory lost at that time. But while almost all the Europeans and Maoris are nominally Christians, support the All Blacks rugby team and have English as a mother tongue (though Maori is also an official language), it's likely that the increasing engagement with their Asian neighbours will challenge their ideas and self-image in the years to come.

New Zealand has transformed itself from the sleepy colonial outpost of the 1950s into a dynamic country whose main cities reflect a fusion of Asian, Pacific and European cultures. Beyond them, the timeless landscape is almost as empty of human habitation and as redolent of myth and legend as when the first people arrived on these shores.

Guy Minder

istockphoto.com/Puschmann

hemis.fr/Gardel

Masses of lupins bring colour to the landscape. | **Te Papa Museum in Wellington explores traditional culture.** | **On the road to Aoraki/Mt Cook.**

A Maori chief by Sydney Parkinson, the artist on Captain Cook's first voyage in 1769.

FLASHBACK

According to archaeological evidence, carbon-14 dating and so on, it seems that the first inhabitants of New Zealand arrived in several waves from Polynesia, at the end of the 13th century. They gradually spread all through the county, reaching the far-off Chatham Islands, 800 km (500 miles) to the east, around 1500.

Maori sagas tell of subsequent landings, such as the Great Migration of the mid-14th century. According to this version, overpopulation and food shortages on Hawaiki, thought to be an island near Tahiti, led to a group of seven ships setting off to find new territory, under the leadership of the great explorer Kupe.

What is certain is that the early Polynesians had the nautical skill and equipment to achieve such epic sea crossings. They had already island-hopped across the Pacific in their sturdy double-hulled vessels, bringing food, plants and animals with them, and this is indeed how dogs, rats, the kumara (a type of sweet potato), taro and yam first came to New Zealand, or Aotearoa as it became known to the Maoris. These early settlers also found a ready source of food in the flightless moa bird, which was hunted to extinction long before the first Europeans arrived on the scene. It is probable that it was the abundance of this vitamin-rich meat that allowed the population to flourish and subsequently spread throughout the North and South Islands.

Rise of Maori Culture

Archaeologists divide the pre-European history of New Zealand into Archaic and Classic Maori phases, though they have no clear idea of when the first, moa-hunting phase developed into the second agriculturalist phase. The fact that the change occurred, however, is thought to be due to the improvement in raising and storing tropical Polynesian crops in what was, after all, a much cooler climate. By the 15th century, different Maori tribes had evolved and they became fiercely competitive with each other for resources and land. Fortified villages were built close to the kumara fields,

Admire a glacier. The mighty **Franz Josef** and **Fox** glaciers are two extraordinary cascades of ice that flow down from the highest point of the Southern Alps almost to sea level.

reflecting both the importance of the crop and the constant threat from inter-tribal wars and skirmishes. At the same time Maori culture reached a notable high point, with a rich oral tradition encompassing storytelling, mythology and religion, and sophisticated techniques in canoe construction, building, weaving and the visual arts. Significantly, the more benevolent climate and easier opportunities for growing crops on North Island meant that the Maori tribes gradually shifted northwards, and when the first Europeans arrived it's thought that around 95 per cent of the population lived there.

A European Encounter

Those first Europeans were led by the Dutch sailor Abel Janszoon Tasman, and sighted the western coast of South Island in December 1642. Tasman—who had already that year discovered Tasmania, the Australian island named after him—was there on behalf of the Dutch East India Company, and his mission was to secure the company's trading rights in the region and find precious metals. The explorer never actually set foot on dry land, however, as a clash between his landing party and the local tribesmen left four Dutch sailors dead. Tasman fled, though not before charting the western coast of the country and calling it Staten Landt, a name that was later changed by the Dutch to Nieuw Zeeland or Nova Zeelandia.

Arrival of the British

The Maori remained untroubled by European intervention for another 127 years, but that would change forever with the arrival of Captain James Cook's ship *Endeavour* in 1769. Cook circumnavigated both the main islands, making accurate maps and proving for the first time that New Zealand wasn't the western part of a huge southern continent as had previously been posited from Tasman's sketchy charts. Cook's visit also made further European interest in the country inevitable.

Much to Cook's surprise his Tahitian interpreter was able to understand the islanders' language. This allowed him and the naturalist Joseph Banks, who accompanied him on his voyages around the southern oceans, substantial access to Maori life and customs, and they were struck by the advanced culture they found, praising the quality of its arts and the sophistication of its tribal structures. That didn't stop Cook claiming New Zealand for Britain without consulting the inhabitants, and then recommending it as a place ripe for British colonization. This was the age of colonial rivalry between Britain and France, and a French expedition under Jean François Marie de Surville had arrived at New Zealand at the same time as Cook. With its recently acquired territory in Australia, Britain was in little doubt as to the strategic and financial benefits of taking New Zealand as well. Formal British control of New Zealand seemed inevitable.

wikimedia.org

Captain Cook by John Webber, displayed in the Te Papa museum.

Sealers and Whalers

The first European immigrants were sealing communities and British and American in the southern waters (between 1810 and 1813, 180,000 sealskins were brought from Macquarie Island), while French whalers settled around Kororareka (now Russell) in the Bay of Islands in the far north of New Zealand. At this stage the Maori welcomed the newcomers, and many of them became absorbed into the new economy as crew members on board whaling ships and customers for trade with the Pakeha, as they called the Europeans. The emergence of this new material wealth enabled them to buy firearms and so carry on their old tribal disputes with a ferocity aided and abetted by modern technology. The so-called Musket Wars raged from 1807 to 1842, and the northern chief Hongi Hika amassed such a huge arsenal of muskets that he was able to dominate much of North Island.

By the 1830s, Maori society had been profoundly affected by its contact with Europeans. The population had been reduced not only because of the enhanced capacity for warfare brought about by the introduction of modern weaponry, but also by the advent of European diseases to which they had no resistance. On top of this, the first missionary station had been established in 1814, and by the mid-19th century almost all the Maori had been converted to Christianity in some form or other. But the most dramatic transformation of all for the indigenous peoples was still to come.

British Colonization

By the late 1830s, the European presence in New Zealand was increasing rapidly. Colonization schemes were being developed by private companies in England such as the New Zealand Association, founded in 1837 by Edward Gibbon Wakefield. Insubordinated European adventurers and intertribal conflict were causing problems, and French settlers were still seen as a potential threat. In the face of all this, the British government decided upon partial annexation. In 1839 it commissioned a naval officer, William Hobson, to carry out the task, but he went beyond his original remit and annexed the entire country. This was achieved via the Treaty of

hemis.fr/Gardel

Waitangi of 1840, under the terms of which 500 Maori chiefs ceded sovereignty to the British crown in return for protection of their rights and land. The correct interpretation of the terms of the treaty are still subject to debate. New Zealand became legally part of New South Wales, and a year later it was declared a separate crown colony in its own right. Hobson was chosen as the first governor.

He was responsible for creating Auckland as the seat of government in 1840, though the capital was moved to Wellington in 1865. When further settlement from Europe was encouraged, the land issue became more severe, while many disputed lands had changed hands during the Musket Wars. Maori rights were soon threatened, and the attempt to establish a native monarchy, after 1852, did not provide a solution. Conflict worsened. By 1860 troops were being used to enforce the purchase of land. The result was war.

Establishing the Nation

The New Zealand Wars lasted throughout the 1860s. Although the Maori tribes who fought weren't conclusively defeated, they were no match for the regular soldiers of the British Army. The ultimate outcome was more land confiscation and further influxes of Europeans, lured by the economic boom that derived from the rich wool trade and the Dunedin gold rush of the 1860s. From 1882, when the first shipment of refrigerated lamb left for England, New Zealand became a major exporter of meat to the mother country.

By the end of the century, New Zealand had been transformed

Commemorating the Treaty of Waitangi in North Island.

Guy Minder

wikimedia.org

Recollections of the pioneers and gold-rush days in modern Dunedin, and of the Maori at Gallipoli.

into a predominantly Anglo-Saxon country, where English was the only language taught in schools and the Maori were virtually marginalized. In 1893, New Zealand was the first country in the world to give women the right to vote. Alongside this radical social approach was a resolutely conservative loyalty to the British crown. New Zealand sent troops to assist Britain during the Boer War, while in World War I more than 100,000 men served overseas on the side of the British,

which, remarkably, amounted to almost 10 per cent of the entire New Zealand population. On the other hand, the war was a defining moment for New Zealand and the courage and resolve shown by its troops as part of the ANZAC contingent at battles in Gallipoli and France boosted the idea of itself as a separate nation. At the peace conference at Versailles, New Zealand was represented by its own delegation, though the government subsequently proved more reluctant than their Australian neighbours to push for full autonomy.

The Modern Era

In 1907 the country had obtained the statute of Dominion. The close ties to England were demonstrated again in 1939, when New Zealand immediately backed up Britain's declaration of war against Germany. But World War II would prove something of a turning point for the country. Its troops once again fought in European theatres of war, but after the Japanese entry into the war in 1941 they served in the Pacific in defence of their own country. With the US as the dominant Allied force in the region it was clear that future security would lie with them, and not the British. In 1947 New Zealand achieved full independence from Britain and four years later joined

ANZUS, a defensive alliance with Australia and the US. This had some unforeseen outcomes, however, as it led the country into subsequent US military actions in the Far East, most controversially in Vietnam. A further realignment of the traditional links with the homeland came with Britain's entry into the European Common Market in 1973, and a century of preferential trading rights over the supply of meat to the mother country came to an end, creating a severe recession in New Zealand's economy.

The election of David Lange's Labour Party in 1984 signalled a change in the attitudes of New Zealanders. The new government was committed to a strict anti-nuclear policy, much to the annoyance of the United States, whose ships were refused entry to ports unless they proved they had no nuclear material on board. The government also made away with the legal barriers that had hitherto prevented the Maoris from undertaking the process leading to the return of or compensation for land taken since 1840 under the conditions of the Treaty of Waitangi. It seemed that New Zealand was at last following its own way in the world.

New Zealand Today

The country has come a long way since its early days as an outpost of England. Although the British monarch is still head of state and republicanism seems to be making little headway, the population is now far more diverse and includes substantial communities from China and the Pacific Rim as well as from western Europe. There are also many more visitors from abroad: the advent of long-distance and lower-priced air travel means that New Zealand welcomes nearly 2.5 million people a year from overseas—in 1960 that figure was just 39,000. The continuing issue of Maori land rights still threatens to erupt in what appears to be a country that's achieved the good life for its citizens. In 2003 a court decision upheld a claim that the Maori were entitled to the nation's seabed and foreshore. Some beach-loving New Zealanders panicked at this and the right-wing National Party was the beneficiary at the ballot box. Since 2009, the Maori and New Zealand flags fly side by side on the anniversary of the Waitangi Treaty.

Since September 2010, several important earthquakes have hit the region of the Canterbury plains, and in particular the historic centre of Christchurch, which was virtually destroyed by a quake of a magnitude of 6.3 on the Richter scale that caused more than 180 victims.

Paved in yellow terracotta, Civic Square is surrounded by distinctive architecture.

ON THE SCENE

North Island, the more populated of the two main islands, boasts delightful colonial cities to explore, along with lots of natural volcanic activity, and the "Winterless North" as the locals call the long, finger-like stretch known as Northland. South Island is wilder, colder and emptier than its sibling. Beyond it to the south is New Zealand's third major landmass, Stewart Island, unscathed by tourism and almost completely under government protection.

North Island

We shall start our tour at Wellington, the nation's capital city.

Wellington

Named after the first Duke of Wellington, New Zealand's capital is also known as the "Windy City" and that's no exaggeration: the wind here can sometimes knock you off your feet. On the bright side, it is delightfully fresh and bracing, and keeps the city relatively free of pollution. Situated at the southwest tip of the North Island, Wellington looks across Cook Strait to the South Island, only 22 km (14 miles) away. Wellington Harbour ranks among the finest in the world: it handles international shipping and is the chief ferry terminus. Beyond the city are New Zealand's oldest zoo, a superb botanical garden, mountaintop panoramas of the capital, and miles of unspoiled beaches.

Many of the 393,000 inhabitants of Wellington live up in the hills around the downtown area and have to climb innumerable flights of steps to get home. You can follow the little alleys and stairways winding up to their quaint gabled cottages and wooden colonial houses. Down in the business district, built on land reclaimed from the harbour, old Wellington is being transformed. If many Wellingtonians have welcomed the 21st-century edge to the city brought by this glass and concrete invasion of modern buildings, it's a cause of regret for those who love the unique higgledy-piggledy character of the place.

R.J. Seddon, prime minister for 13 years, in front of the Beehive.

wikimedia.org

Lambton Quay and Cable Car

Wellington's main commercial street used to run along the waterfront, but reclamation has pushed the land out. Plaques set into the pavement mark the old shoreline. The picturesque and always popular cable car goes from here up to Kelburn hill and Wellington's Botanic Garden for excellent views of the inner harbour and central city. The first cable car began in 1902 and was steam powered; the current ones (1978) run on electricity and were designed in Switzerland.

Botanic Garden

At the upper cable car terminal, a lookout offers magnificent views of the city. Nearby, the **Cable Car Museum** houses one of the original steam cars and an exhibition on cable cars around the world.

From here, paths lead through various parts of the Botanic Garden, with its outstanding display of native plants, to beautiful Lady Norwood Rose Garden and the Begonia House. At night, especially after rain, the sector between the Duck Pond and Glen Road, along the Pukatea stream, is pure magic, with thousands of flickering fireflies flittering about.

When it's clear, stargazers should check out the **Carter Observatory** to see the southern hemisphere's night sky (Tuesday and Saturday). There's also a planetarium and displays on astronomy. A stone's throw away is the **Thomas King Observatory**, which allows you to view the surface of the sun in safety.

Parliament District

Down between Molesworth, Hill and Bowen streets, three buildings make up the Parliament complex. The neoclassical main building (1922) housing the **Legislative Chambers** loses out to the more beguiling neo-Gothic **Parliamentary Library** (1899), whose arches and spires bring a hint of frivolity to the seat of national government.

Visit a museum. In Wellington, **Te Papa** is a cutting-edge, five-storey celebration of New Zealand history, culture, geology and geography. The **Canterbury Museum** in Christchurch has a superb collection of Maori artefacts and items relating to New Zealand's role in Antarctic exploration. The **Auckland Museum** boasts a first-rate display on Polynesian and Maori culture.

The rotunda of the Executive Wing, designed by Sir Basil Spence and completed in 1981, is familiarly known as "the Beehive".

Beyond the Parliament complex is the **National Library**. The **National Archives**, a block away on Mulgrave Street, house a fascinating collection of books, manuscripts, photos and maps of early New Zealand. Not to be missed is the Treaty of Waitangi in the Constitution Room. Dating from 1840, it made the Maoris subjects of the British crown; it is now on permanent display. Entrance is free.

On the same street, **Old St Paul's Cathedral** (1866) was designed by the vicar-cum-architect Frederick Thatcher. His greatest achievement was to adapt the early English style to the requirements of a wooden building, which makes the interior especially striking as the Gothic features more familiarly seen in stone appear here in dark, native timber: kauri, rimu, matai and totara. Also noteworthy are the stained-glass windows.

The **Old Government Building** (1876) at the north end of Lambton Quay, below the Beehive, is one of the largest wooden edifices in the world, constructed almost entirely of native kauri wood. It now serves as the Faculty of Law.

Museum of Wellington City & Sea

Originally a warehouse, the museum on Queens Wharf is filled with state-of-the-art displays recounting the town's history. A film on a giant screen relates the Maori creation myths, while another documents the *Wahine* disaster of 1968, when one of the ferries between Wellington and South Island sank with the loss of 51 lives.

Civic Square

The new waterfront development is an attractive place to stroll, sample restaurants and view the harbour scene. Begin at the New Town Hall in Civic Square, where bronze palm trees contribute a tropical note. Here you'll find the city library, a Fine Arts museum (with temporary exhibitions of contemporary art with Maori and Pacific sections) and the Tourist Office.

hemis.fr / Heeb

wikimedia.org

flickr.com / Kahari

National Museum
Te Papa Tongarewa

Further south along the waterfront, Te Papa Tongarewa, known as Our Place, occupies a purpose-built five-storey complex. The guiding concept of its designers is that education and amusement belong together, with the result that it combines classical and interactive displays and organizes temporary exhibitions. The most important section is devoted to Maori history and culture, with, in particular, a large war canoe, a meeting house and granary, all superbly carved. On two floors you can discover the natural environment and the consequences of human activity on the flora and fauna, and admire in passing the world's biggest ammonite, the only giant squid ever displayed in a museum, and one of the canon from Captain Cook's ship *Endeavour*. Other sections present the country's cultural mosaic and a collection of fine arts.

Other Museums

Wellington has an interesting collection of smaller speciality museums.

Take the cable car for thrilling views over the city and harbour. | Katherine Mansfield's birthplace. | The thumbprint logo of Te Papa museum has become a beloved symbol.

The **Colonial Cottage Museum**, 68 Nairn Street, occupies the oldest building in the city centre, dating from 1858 and focusing on colonial life. It was built by a young carpenter, William Wallis, who lived there with his wife and seven of their ten children.

A short walk north of here at 187 Vivian Street, the **National Tattoo Museum** looks at traditional and contemporary tattoo practises and their universal history.

The **New Zealand Film Archive** at 84 Taranaki Street holds a copy of every movie, TV newsreels and documentaries made in the country, and you can see them free of charge.

Katherine Mansfield's Birthplace is at 25 Tinakori Road in the Thorndon suburb, a 10-minute walk north of the Parliament buildings. As you might expect, it pays homage to New Zealand's first great author. You can visit the house and garden.

Adjacent to the premises of Peter Jackson's Weta film production company, a mini-museum has been set up at the **Weta Cave**, on the corner of Camperdown Road and Weka Street in the Miramar district north of the airport. Here you can watch a 20-minute film showing behind-the-scenes secrets, and see some of the props and displays from the movies, including a model of Gollum.

Beyond the City

Heading along the highway that starts at Oriental Bay and meanders for about 40 km (25 miles) along the coast, you will see an enormous expanse of shore, from the sand beaches of chic suburbia to jagged rocks and rolling grey sea. At Oriental Bay itself, be sure to make a detour up to **Mt Victoria lookout** for panoramic views of the city and harbour.

Otari–Wilton's Bush

In the suburb of Wilton, 5 km (3 miles) northwest of the centre, is the Otari Native Botanic Garden and Wilton's Bush Reserve, the largest collection of local plant life. The flora of these islands developed for 90 million years independently from the rest of the world, and so the plants displayed here are unique. The forest has some ancient rimu and rata trees, up to 800 years old. A walkway takes you through the tree canopy, 18 m (60 ft) over the ground.

Zealandia

Like the country's plant life, its fauna is also special, because of the islands' long isolation. Until relatively recently insects, reptiles, sea mammals and birds were the only living fauna to be found on the islands. The natural reserve of Zealandia, in a valley overlooking the western suburbs of Karori, 10 minutes from

Wellington, has been fenced in to protect reintroduced endemic species from predators. This gives you the chance to see tuatara, hihi, kaka, kakariki and (at night) kiwis. The educational centre traces the effects of human impact on New Zealands natural environment and introduces you to a moa larger than life.

Wellington Zoo

New Zealand's oldest zoo is in Newtown, a southern suburb. In addition to native animals, it has numerous species from all over the world, including endangered Sumatran tigers. Still extant and unique to New Zealand is the Campbell teal, a.flightless, nocturnal duck.

Central North Island

The large central area of North Island offers diverse pleasures. Many of them are natural wonders, ranging from spectacular crater lakes and geysers to underground cave systems and thermal seawater that bubbles up through the beach. But whether it's Art Deco architecture or some of the best vineyards in the southern hemisphere, the man-made alternatives also have much to offer.

A proud line-up of restored Art Deco houses, the hallmark of Napier. | Cone-shaped Mt Ngauruhoe in Tongariro NP.

hemis.fr/Gardel

istockphoto.com/Piskunov

Hawke's Bay

The area is famous for its fine, sunny weather, and the vineyards that were planted here to capitalize on it. But visitors will also find themselves spending time in the delightful main towns of Napier and Hastings, with their range of Art Deco buildings.

Napier

Long before Captain Cook discovered Hawke's Bay in 1769, the Maoris had found Napier to be a favourable site, with plenty of food available. The Otatara *pa* (fortified settlement), with rebuilt barricades, dates from those times. By 1838 Europeans had established a trading base, which evolved into a flourishing town, but in 1931 a severe earthquake and resulting fire destroyed most of it. The reconstructed town is a handsome ensemble of pastel-coloured Art Deco buildings.

Marine Parade, the pretty seaside boulevard lined with Norfolk pine trees and sunken gardens, gives the town the air of an old-fashioned English resort. Strung out along it are most of Napier's diversions. The **New Zealand National Aquarium** ripples with sharks, crocodiles, and piranha. In the **Kiwi House**, you can see the beloved national bird in a darkened enclosure; the animals are more active after feeding time, at 2 p.m.

Also on Marine Parade is the **Hawke's Bay Museum**, whose audio-visual show can fill you in on the earthquake of 1931. You can also admire Maori artefacts and objects from the colonial era.

Call in at the **New Zealand Wine Centre**, in the Iconic AMP Building, 1 Shakespeare Road, for a virtual tour of the vineyards and a tasting.

The Vineyards

The Hawke's Bay area has more than 90 vineyards ranged in a wide arc to the west and southwest of Napier. A scenic "wine road" leads from winery to winery, and you can join one of the group tours from Napier. Alternatively, you can rent a bike and cycle, as many of the vineyards are just a few kilometres outside towns like Napier and Hastings.

Hastings

Hastings is Napier's twin city to the south, where there's a brewery to visit as well as several wineries. Like Napier, it is partly built in Art Deco style, with additions of Spanish-mission architecture — be sure to see the local Opera House, the most striking example of this California-influenced style.

If you visit the region between October and end April, you'll be able to take in the spectacle at the **Cape Kidnappers** gannet colony, where unperturbed by onlookers the large birds nest on the mainland, making use of all the driftwood and other materials thrown up during storms.

Tongariro National Park

Established in 1887, this is New Zealand's oldest national park, situated at the very centre of North Island. It was an area of special religious significance to the local Maori tribes and for this reason was given to the nation by chief Te Heuheu Tukino IV as a means of preserving it from the European land-grab taking place at that time. The terrain here is as varied as it is spectacular: the mighty volcanoes of Mt Ruapehu, Mt Tongariro and the conical Mt Ngauruhoe are still active, and have created crater lakes filled with brilliantly coloured water, while virgin rainforest and semi-arid plateaux are set against peaks of ice and snow. It's little wonder that the film director Peter Jackson chose this as the location for some of the most dramatic scenes in *Lord of the Rings*, where it stands in for Mordor and Mt Doom, the Mountain of Fire. There are many long walking trails you can follow around the park, but a superb one-day hike is the famous **Tongariro Crossing**, which offers marvellous vistas and a satisfying sense of having experienced the park to the full.

Waitomo Caves

Around 150 km (93 miles) north of Tongariro, the underground limestone caves and strange limestone formations at Waitomo (literally "water shaft") provide one of North Island's most intriguing natural wonders. There are more than 300 individual caves, though the best of them can be viewed in a 45-minute guided tour. This takes you via a paved walkway past a series of extraordinary shapes—sculpted by acid made from a combination of rainwater and carbon dioxide that dissolves the soft limestone—into the Cathedral Cave and then onto a boat for a magical view of **Glowworm Cave**. The darkness of this cave is illumined by what looks like thousands of tiny stars, but are in fact the *Arachnocampa luminosa,* or a fungus gnat that glows in the larval stage.

Bay of Plenty

As its name suggests, the Bay of Plenty is a place of richness: the agricultural land here is fertile, the communities prosperous and the climate benevolent. It was so named by Captain Cook, who found several Maori settlements in the area and was impressed by their affluence and friendliness. Today, it's one of the fastest-growing parts in the country, drawing young families seeking a laid-back lifestyle.

NEW ZEALAND'S MIDDLE EARTH

It was only natural that when New Zealand-born film director Peter Jackson was given the role of filming Tolkien's epic fantasy trilogy *The Lord of the Rings*, he should look to his native landscape to provide a suitably magical backdrop. Where else, Jackson pointed out, would you find such a variety of dramatic scenery in such a small area? And so the great Ngauruhoe volcano in Tongariro National Park became the grim Mt Doom at the heart of Mordor; and Matamata, near Rotorua, was the setting for Hobbiton, home of the Hobbits. This still has some of the original movie sets in place, namely the hillside holes where the Hobbits live, but fans will also recognize the Party Tree, a huge radiata pine, and the nearby lake.

On South Island, check out Mt Sunday in the Southern Alps, transformed into Edoras, capital of Rohan. Around Queenstown, several *Lord of the Rings* sites include Skipper's Canyon, The Remarkables range of hills and Arrowtown. Queenstown has several companies specializing in LOTR tourism, some of which use guides who worked for the location teams during filming. Indeed, the trilogy inspired a whole new tourist industry, as film buffs came to New Zealand in search of the original locations of Middle-Earth. More than 160 different locations were used, and tourist offices throughout the country are always keen to offer advice on how to get to them.

The final part of the trilogy, *The Return of King*, swept the board by winning 11 Oscars at the 2004 Academy Awards ceremony in Hollywood. An Oscar for the "Most Spectacular Country in a Motion Picture" would clearly have gone to New Zealand.

Thanks to carbonated gases, the Champagne Pool at Waiotapu is as fizzy as a glass of bubbly.

Tauranga

At Tauranga, at the western end of the bay, life revolves around the kiwi fruit, grown in the surrounding area and shipped out from the port. Some of the first Maori to reach New Zealand landed here; the name means "safe anchorage for canoes". A replica canoe, *Te Awanui*, is displayed near the town centre.

The **Compass Community Village** on 17th Avenue contains an interesting collection of restored period buildings, with relics from the gold-mining era and various vintage vehicles. But be sure also to visit the **Elms Mission Station House** on Mission Street. Built between 1835 and 1847, it's one of the oldest houses in the country. The interior has original dark-wood furnishings, including the table at which British officers dined before the bloody Battle of Gate Pa at the height of the New Zealand Wars in 1864: only one of them survived.

There are plenty of sporting activities to be enjoyed here, from swimming with dolphins to white-water rafting and skydiving. For the best beaches, head to **Mt Maunganui**, a 232-m (761-ft) extinct volcano on the headland just across the bay from Tauranga. The sea here is especially popular with surfers (the national surf championships are held here), while the mount provides some excellent hiking trails with great views from the summit.

Rotorua

"Sulphur City" is a popular name for Rotorua south of Tauranga—you'll notice the smell as soon as you draw near. There's considerable thermal activity throughout much of New Zealand and above all in the Rotorua area, a major safety valve for various subterranean upheavals. As a result, there are hot pools and fumaroles in every direction, while even the manicured English restraint of the Government Gardens is marked by exotically steaming thermal pools. The gardens were founded as a spa retreat in 1908; now, the mock-Tudor bathhouse is home to the **Rotorua Museum of Art and History**. Fascinating exhibits describe the history and culture of the Arawa tribe with a fine collection of artefacts, the history of Rotorua and the extraordinarily powerful volcanic eruption of Mt Tarawera in 1886, as well as the involvement of the 28 Maori Battalion in World War II.

At the southern exit of town, **Whakarewarewa** (generally shortened to Whaka), is the best-known thermal area. **Te Puia park** features several active spouts, but the star turn is **Pohutu** ("splash"), a temperamental fellow that erupts 15 to 20 times a day spurting boiling hot water at least 20 m (65 ft) into the air. The park also includes a **Maori model village**, a carved meeting house and a Kiwi House, where you can see the country's emblematic bird. Various performances are organized and you can sample a *hangi*, the traditional Maori meal. Similar themed evenings take place in the Maori "villages" of Whakarewarewa, Tamai and Matariki.

Waimangu

In the direction of Taupo, to the south, the superb **Waimangu Crater**, a pale blue warm-water lake, was formed by the Mt Tarawera eruption in 1886. Here, as at nearby Wai-O-Tapu, you can see natural boiling water, bubbling mud flats and other natural phenomena. **Wai-O-Tapu**, known for its Champagne Pool full of bubbles, also has the most punctual geyser in the country: Lady Knox erupts every morning at 10.15 and gushes for an hour.

Taupo

Taupo lies at the northeast corner of Lake Taupo, the largest in the whole country with an area of 606 sq km (234 sq miles) and source of New Zealand's longest river, the **Waikato**, an unusual bright blue colour. The serene lake—reckoned to be the world's trout fishing capital—was formed by a cataclysmic eruption that took place 26,500 years ago. In town, the **Taupo Museum** is worth a visit, with a fine collection of old photographs of the area, a canoe, a traditional Maori meeting house and an art gallery.

There are facilities for all kinds of water sports, from canoeing to wakeboarding.

Coromandel Peninsula

The rugged, densely forested peninsula is a popular holiday retreat, with plenty of opportunities for hiking, cycling, fishing or just lazing on the beach. The

The Sky Tower, with the Sky Walk right up near the clouds.

main town is **Thames**, its quiet streets lined with wooden houses built during the gold-mining days of the 19th century. Most visitors call in briefly on their way to the charming little town of **Coromandel**, a gold mining centre from 1852 to the 1920s, facing an island-speckled bay. Like Colville further north, it attracts people in search of an alternative lifestyle and is particularly noted for its crafts. It makes an excellent base for exploring the north end of the peninsula, with splendid, lonely beaches. For an unfor-

gettable beach experience, **Hot Water Beach**, on the east coast, is hard to beat. The water here lives up to its name, and for a couple of hours either side of low tide you can dig a hole in the sand and relax in your own thermal pool.

From the nearby resort of **Hahei**, a track leads you to the big stone arch of Cathedral Cove, carved out by erosion from the high white cliffs.

Auckland

This is New Zealand's New York, the commercial and cultural capital of the nation, though it only lasted for a mere 25 years as the actual capital city in the mid-19th century before this status was bestowed upon Wellington. It is the country's biggest city, with a population of some 1.4 million people, including the largest concentration of Polynesians in the world. But this cosmopolitan, thriving seaport has also held on to its easy-going atmosphere. The high-rise buildings are interspersed with squares with modern sculptures, green lawns and open parkland, creating a feeling of spaciousness.

Getting around the central district is relatively easy. Queen Street runs like a spine along the middle of downtown Auckland, while around it are various other reminders of the city's British foundations, like Victoria Park,

Albert Park and, at the Waitemata Harbour end of Queen Street, Queen Elizabeth II Square.

Waitemata Harbour

Harbour Bridge spans the 1,020-m (3,346-ft) gap over Waitemata Harbour and joins the main city to the beach resort of Takapuna in the suburbs. From the bridge you'll see **Westhaven Boat Harbour**, one of the world's biggest pleasure-yacht basins. You can bungy jump from the bridge.

Voyager New Zealand Maritime Museum

In the "City of Sails", as Auckland is familiarly known, a visit to the museum on Viaduct Harbour is a must. Sea lovers can study the country's seafaring past, back to the times of the Polynesian migrations. The many boats on display include a large outrigger canoe that was constructed recently using ancient Maori methods, and successfully sailed across the Pacific. In the gallery devoted to Sir Peter Blake (2948–2001), the NZL32 *Black Magic* won the 1995 America's Cup. You can join a harbour cruise and sail on one of three museum ships.

Queen Street

Auckland's main shopping thoroughfare cuts right up the centre of town from the wharves. To the

right you'll notice the restored **Customs House**, now packed with boutiques. Off to the right down Victoria Street needles the **Sky Tower**, 328 m (1,076 ft) high, offering thrilling panoramas over the harbour and the city. You can make a cable-controlled base jump from the SkyJump or stroll around the edge at the SkyWalk, at 192 m (630 ft). Further up Queen Street, **Karangahape Road** (K'Road for short) crosses Queen Street and is full of second-hand outlets and vintage shops.

Auckland Art Gallery

On the east side of Queen Street next to Albert Park, the gallery (Toi o Tamaki) displays New Zealand's most important collection of national and international art. They include paintings by artists who arrived with Captain Cook through to Charles F. Goldie's portraits of Maori from the turn of the century and more modern perspectives by artists such as Rita Angus, Tony Fomison and Russell Clark. Temporary exhibitions are organized.

Albert Park

On a small hill overlooking the gallery, Albert Park is pretty and green, full of statues, and affords good views of the city and harbour. Next door are the buildings of Auckland University and the 1926 **Clock Tower**.

istockphoto.com/Heyward

Auckland Museum
The vast park called the Auckland Domain is the site of the imposing, colonnaded marble Auckland Museum, housing the world's biggest collection of Maori art and artefacts, including, on the ground floor, the 25-m (82-ft) war canoe *Te Toki a Tapiri* and the elaborately decorated Hotunui meeting house, as well as an exhibition on the childhood of Pakeha (New Zealanders of European origin), design and decorative arts. On the next floor are displays on New Zealand's natural wonders and a children's activity centre, and at the top of the building the War Stories display deals with New Zealand at war from the 19th century to the present. A performance of Maori singing and dancing takes place three times a day.

Parnell
On the east side of the Domain, the once rundown Parnell area received a radical dose of urban renewal in the 1980s. Lots of attractive old buildings in various styles were revealed and have now been restored to their former elegance. It has become a major tourist shopping area, with bou-

wikimedia.org

A monarch on milkweed. | **The male brown kiwi sits on the eggs for the 85 days of their incubation.**

See a volcano. On North Island's west coast, **Mt Taranaki** (or Mt Egmont) has acted as a stand-in for Japan's Mt Fuji in films. **Mt Eden**, south of Auckland, provides great views of the city and its surroundings. **Rangitoto Island**, part of the Hauraki Islands, is a volcano that erupted from the sea 600 years ago. At 2,797 m (9,176 ft), **Mt Ruapehu**, in Tongariro National Park, offers a thrilling crater rim circuit and endless vistas.

tiques of all sorts, art galleries, cafés and fine restaurants. A French market, **La Cigale**, is held at 69 St George's Bay Road, on Saturday and Sunday mornings.

The beautiful **Parnell Rose Gardens**, also known as Sir Dove Myer Robinson Park, are definitely worth a visit. The 5,000 bushes are best seen between October and April.

Volcanoes
Auckland is located within an area of around 50 dormant volcanoes. The most accessible is the 196-m (643-ft) **Mt Eden** (Maungawhau), an extinct volcano just south of the centre. The drive up provides superb views of the city and harbour, and you can look down at the green crater. Across the harbour, in the suburb of

Devonport, **Mt Victoria** offers similarly spectacular 360-degree views. Guided tours take you on the traces of the Maoris, here and in other places around the city.

One Tree Hill
This 182-m (600-ft) hill 5 km (3 miles) southeast of Auckland is the site of a former Maori village, with an obelisk raised by Sir John Logan Campbell, "the father of Auckland". He is buried on the summit of this volcanic cone. The hill's name came from a pohutukawa tree that was chopped down by a European settler in 1852. A Monterey pine planted in its place by Logan Campbell was attacked by Maori protesters and suffered a similar fate to the original in 2000; so now people call it None-Tree Hill.

Auckland Zoo
In Western Springs, the environment-friendly zoo has a vast section (Te Wao Nui) devoted to New Zealand fauna (and flora), with some 60 species in six "natural" habitats. Most visitors make a beeline for the Kiwi & Tuatara House, to observe the birds in "moon-lit" conditions, grubbing for worms with their long beaks.

Museum of Transport and Technology (MOTAT)
Also in the Western Springs area, this museum is located on two

different sites linked by a tram (with a stop at the Zoo). The building on Great North Road houses a collection of vintage cars, rail cars and a tramway. The Meola Road site displays New Zealand's biggest collection of airplanes, and there's also a Victorian village with a dozen 19th-century buildings.

Kelly Tarlton's Antarctic Encounter & Underwater World

Established by the diver Kelly Tarlton in 1985 inside Auckland's former storm-water holding tanks at Orakei Wharf, 6 km (4 miles) to the east of the city, this is a huge interactive re-creation of two very different environments. The Antarctic Encounter includes a model of explorer Robert Falcon Scott's hut used on his doomed expedition to the South Pole in 1911–12, and you can ride on a Snowcat through a penguin colony. The aquarium has pools for sharks and rays viewed from a tunnel. If you're brave you can swim among them.

Around Auckland

Most of the many excursions from Auckland can be enjoyed on day trips. To the north is Avondale, and the Greenstone Factory, where you can see how New Zealand's nephrite (a variety of jade) is cut and worked into polished stones and pendants.

Waitakere Scenic Drive

West from Auckland are the Waitakere Ranges, rising to 500 m (1,640 ft). The delightful scenic drive meanders through lush green hills and smart suburban settlements. At a narrow viewpoint on high, you see the Tasman Sea on one side, the Pacific on the other. Past the Henderson area and wine-growing region, you'll come to rolling green hills and pastures. At Warkworth visit **SheepWorld**, a theme park with sheep-shearing and sheep-dog demonstrations.

Hauraki Gulf

The 47 islands of the Hauraki Gulf are just a stone's throw away from the big city life. **Waiheke**, a half-hour ferry ride from Auckland, has sandy beaches, top-quality vineyards and a relaxed lifestyle; on **Great Barrier Island**, the largest in the group, you can go mountain biking, surfing, sea kayaking or relax on pristine beaches. Not to be missed, **Rangitoto** is the nearest island to Auckland as well as the youngest in the group—it emerged from the sea in a volcanic explosion around 600 years ago. It has the country's biggest pohutukawa forest. The hour-long hike to the summit of the volcano is rewarded by a loop walk around the crater rim, great views and the chance to visit a set of lava caves.

Northland

This 350-km (217-mile) finger of
land is often called the Winterless
North, benefiting from a year-
round mild climate and, at the top
end, an area which reaches into
the tropics. It's also packed with
natural wonders, from fern trees
and huge kauris to the seemingly
infinite sands on the coast, which
earn it another nickname: "the
land of a thousand beaches". In
the north lies Cape Reinga, so
desolate that the most hardened
traveller may feel tempted to
believe that it is, indeed, the
"leaping-off place of the spirits"
spoken of in Maori legend.

Bay of Islands

A paradise for sailing, kayaking
and big game fishing, the idyllic
bay of 144 islands is a "drowned
river system"—an area where the
sea has inundated a series of river
valleys. The higher ground pokes
through the water, giving a won-
derful panorama of mangroves,
sea and land. Don't miss a sailing
trip around the bay, to spot dolphins or to see the Hole in the
Rock.

Paihia

Paihia makes an excellent base
for excursions to the bay. The
town traces its history back to
1823, when Reverend Henry
Williams established New Zealand's third mission station here.

St Paul's Church (1925) stands as a fond memorial to the minister and his brother, Bishop William Williams. Moored at Waitangi Bridge, the three-masted barque *Tui* built in 1890 now serves as a restaurant and a shipwreck museum.

Waitangi

Appropriately, Waitangi means "Wailing Waters". This is where the Maoris signed the controversial treaty of 1840 by which the British assumed sovereignty over New Zealand. Visit **Treaty House**, built in 1832 for the British resident James Busby, now a museum. A flagstaff in front marks the spot where the treaty was signed. An impressive Maori meeting house (*whare runanga*), erected for the centennial celebrations in 1940, stands across the lawn. It is decorated with remarkable carvings representing many Maori tribes. Also see the Ngatokimatawhaorua war canoe, carved from a huge kauri trunk. Demonstrations of haka and other Maori chants and dance take place every 60 or 90 minutes.

Among the pleasant walks in the bay area, follow the 5-km (3-mile) trail through the **Waitangi Mangrove Forest**. on a raised walkway to the Haruru Falls. The salt swamp where mangrove thrive supports a variety of fish and bird life.

Russell

Regular ferry services link Paihia to Russell across the bay. This quiet little settlement of charming wooden houses facing the harbour used to have a much more sparkly reputation. Grog and girls were the main attractions in the good old days when it was a whaling port known by the Maori name of Kororareka.

Pompallier House incorporates part of the original pisé (mud, ash and clay) building° constructed for the French Catholic missionary, Bishop Jean-Baptiste Pompallier; he installed the mission's printing presses here. The venerable **Christ Church** (1836) is the oldest surviving church in the country; Charles Darwin contributed money towards its construction. The **Russell Museum** displays a superb scale model of Cook's ship, *Endeavour*, and mementoes of Kororareka's racier days.

Kerikeri

Surrounded by orchards, 20 km (12 miles) northwest of Waitangi, the town was home to New Zealand's first mission, set up in 1819. Built in 1822 on the banks of the river, **Kemp House**, drenched in flowers, is the most ancient surviving building in the country. A missionary family lived there till 1848. It can be visited on guided tours. Next door is the basalt Stone Store, dating from 1836.

Ninety Mile Beach

The great arc of Ninety Mile Beach is so impressive that you won't be tempted to question the exaggerated claim for its length (really only 60 miles). The ocean hems you in on one side, while on the other is a wall of storm-fingered dunes. You can drive (4x4) or take a bus tour to the northern tip—Maori tales and a visit to the **Ancient Kauri Kingdom** included. Black rocks and seagulls mark the end of the land.

Omapere and Opononi

These twin towns together form a popular beach resort, enhanced by a long stretch of white sand. At Opononi Wharf you can catch a water taxi to the giant sand dunes on the far side of the harbour for dune surfing on boogie boards.

Waipoua Forest

Kauri thickets that once covered much of Northland; 99 per cent were felled for their wood, but three-quarters of the survivors grow here. The kauri grows slowly to a height of 50 m (164 ft) and can live for 2,000 years. At Matakohe, 50 km (30 miles) to the south, the **Kauri Museum** will tell you all there is to know about the great tree and its exploitation.

Cabbage trees (*Cordyline australis*) and ancient kauris (*Agathis australis*).

hemis.fr/Heeb

istockphoto.com/McKie

Diversity around Lake Wanaka, from laven-
der and vineyards to snowy peaks.

South Island

The dramatic Southern Alps run almost the whole length of South Island in a snow-capped ridge, with Aoraki/ Mt Cook, the highest of the Alps, at the centre of one of the country's finest parks. In the southwest, Fiordland is a haunting world of wild valleys, soaring mountains and startlingly blue water, so remote that only experienced hikers penetrate its virgin bushland.

The North

Many people approach the South Island by the inter-island ferry across the Cook Strait from Wellington to Picton. They may never get much further south, as there is so much to see and do: exploring the bays of the Marlborough Sounds by boat; hiking the popular Queen Charlotte or Abel Tasman tracks; or making an excursion to Kaikoura to see the dolphins and whales.

Picton

Picton is an attractive, sleepy port tucked into the folds of Queen Charlotte Sound; most people just drive through, heading for elsewhere. At the harbour you can look around the remains of the *Edwin Fox*, a 48-m (157-ft) East Indiaman built in Bengal in 1853. It was used as a troop carrier in the Crimean War, transported convicts to Australia, and then carried settlers to New Zealand.

Marlborough Wine Country

Around Blenheim, 28 km (17 miles) south of Picton, this has become New Zealand's top wine-producing region. You can sample some of its highly regarded Sauvignon Blanc and Pinot Noir at wine tasting sessions held in about 40 vineyards.

Marlborough Sounds

Picton makes a good base for explorations of the beautiful bays, coves and islands of the sounds, though for easier access to more remote areas such as the magnificent Pelorus Sound you might consider staying in a smaller settlement such as **Havelock**. The best way to appreciate the sounds is by boat; several cruise boat companies and water taxis operate out of Picton and Havelock, and you can take a trip on the regular mail boat, explore the area by kayak or swim with the dolphins. There are some excellent walking trails offering marvellous views.

Queen Charlotte Track

The 71-km (44-mile) track, a 3–5-day trip, runs from Ship Cove, one of Captain Cook's bases during his voyages in the 1770s, to Anakiwa. The track leads through woods and over high ridges affording splendid coastal scenery of Queen Charlotte Sound and Kenepuru Sound. Water taxis ply between Picton and Ship Cove, making several stops, and day trips are possible. The track is considered one of the best mountain bike tours in the country.

Nydia Track
Lonelier and wilder, this track starts at Kaiuma Bay and ends 27 km (17 miles) further at Duncan Bay (count 2 days). Best reached from Havelock, it leads hikers through virgin forest and open pasture, with breathtaking views from the Kaiuma Saddle and Nydia Saddle.

Nelson
Overlooking Tasman Bay, Nelson is officially the sunniest place in New Zealand. A spire at the top of Botanical Hill in the Botanic Gardens proclaims that it is also the geographical centre, though scientists have now calculated that this is really 35 km (22 miles) to the southwest.

If you can drag yourself away from the beaches, look around the lively town, which has become something of an artists' colony over the years and now has more than its fair share of art galleries, glass-blowing workshops and potteries. The **Suter Art Gallery**, located in the fine Victorian-era Queen's Gardens, puts on temporary exhibitions of local art along with examples from its permanent collection of works by earlier artists such as the watercolourist John Gully.

Broadgreen Historic House, 27 Nayland Road, built in 1855, and the **Founders Heritage Park** are reminders of early times.

The biggest new attraction in town is an altogether showier affair: the **Classic World of Wearable Art and Cars Museum (WOW)** brings together avant-garde clothing design and around 50 vintage cars under one roof.

New Zealand's Narnia. Director Andrew Adamson chose his home country as the setting for the movie *Narnia*, inspired by C.S. Lewis's *Chronicles of Narnia*. Many scenes were filmed in an Auckland studio, but the hills and forests were perfect locations for the outside shots. The Camp of the White Witch was set up beneath the trees of Woodhill Forest, an hour's drive northwest of Auckland, while the Great Battle was fought on Flock Hill, in the Southern Alps of the South Island. The karst landscape of limestone rocks can be reached by the Arthur's Pass Highway between Christchurch and Greymouth. The Elephant Rocks where Aslan's Camp was sited are near Duntroon. The magnificent castle of Cair Paravel was generated by computer, with images superimposed on the cliffs of Purakaunui Bay in the Catlins between Dunedin and Invercargill.

Abel Tasman National Park

At the end of a range of limestone and marble hills, the park is popular for walking tours and sea kayaking. The interior is riddled with caves and potholes, while the coast is dotted with secluded beaches of golden sand and bright blue bays against a backdrop of superb tropical forest. The scenic and popular **Coastal Track** takes three to four days to walk in its entirety. Some sections involve detours during high tides. You can also explore the coastline by kayak or water taxi.

Golden Bay

This is the place where the first Europeans set foot in New Zealand, when Abel Tasman landed in 1642. Four of his crew were killed by the local Ngati Tumatakokiri tribe and Tasman fled.

Te Waikoropupu or Pupu Springs is a sacred place for the Maori people, notable for the remarkable clarity of the water and the volume of water discharged: 14,000 litres per second.

Farewell Spit forms the northern boundary of the bay; it is the longest stretch of dunes in the world, more than 30 km (18 miles) in length. Only part of this wildlife sanctuary is accessible.

Kaikoura

On the east coast some 150 km (93 miles) south of Picton, this

Guy Minder

Guy Minder

The crystalline waters of Pupu Springs. | Kaikoura whale on wall.

picturesque little town is set against the dramatic backdrop of the Seaward Kaikoura Ranges, which are snowcapped in winter. The town developed as a whaling station in the 19th century, but it is now better known for its whale watching opportunities, as well as the chance to swim with dolphins and seals or sail out to see albatross and petrel. Sperm whales and dolphins swim offshore throughout the year, while migratory humpback whales pass by in winter, and you can see killer whales in summer.

On the road to the sea lion colony at Point Kean, the pink **Fyffe House** (1842) is a reminder of the town's whaling past: its foundations are made of whale bone. To learn more about the town's history, visit the **Kaikoura Museum** on Ludstone Road.

Christchurch

The South Island's largest city (population 372,600) is situated inland on the fertile Canterbury Plains; the province rates as the country's chief grain producer, and tender Canterbury lamb is world-famous. Christchurch was founded in 1850 as an Anglican stronghold in England's Antipodean colony, a project inspired by the Canterbury Association, which had been formed at the Oxford University college after which the city is named. With its old greystone buildings, Victorian Gothic architecture, neat gardens and punting on the Avon River, Christchurch evokes the very spirit of England. But a devastating earthquake on February 22, 2011, changed the city's destiny: most of the centre, especially around the cathedral, is a danger zone, still fenced off for security

Though much of Christchurch is awaiting rebuilding, the Antarctic Centre is open for visits. | An avenue of trees in Hagley Park, laid out in the 1850s.

istockphoto.com/Wurditsch

istockphoto.com/Mckie

reasons, and all the more so because of recurring aftershocks. The big quake caused the death of an estimated 182 people. Many of the museums and galleries had to be closed. Some want to raze the centre and rebuild it from zero, other associations are fighting to preserve historic monuments. In any case, nothing will ever be the same as before. For up-to-date information on the situation, consult the Tourist Office site: www.christchurchnz.com

Canterbury Museum
The museum is located in a neo-Gothic gem by Benjamin Woolfield Mountfort (who had completed the magnificent cathedral) and dates from 1882. It's situated on the edge of **Hagley Park** and its botanic garden. Since the earthquake some parts of the museum have been closed and others modified, for instance to make a temporary home for works from the Art Museum, which had to be closed.

Iwi Tawhito Whenua Hou (Ancient People, New Land) is a gallery devoted to the first Polynesians in New Zealand. It also covers the arrival of the European colonists and includes a reconstruction of an old Christchurch street.

Upstairs, exhibits document Christchurch's associations with Antarctic exploration, and several rooms are devoted to natural history — geology, dinosaurs and so on.

International Antarctic Centre
This is one of the city's main attractions, located near the airport. Here you can see what life is and was like at the South Pole; there are penguins, and you can take a 15-minute ride in a Hägglund, a five-tonne buggy normally used for travelling over ice.

Air Force Museum
About 10 minutes from the city centre, to the southwest, this museum displays around 30 planes documenting New Zealand's airborne military history. The programme includes war souvenirs, a simulator and a visit (with a fee) of the hangar where the planes are restored.

Around Christchurch
From the Canterbury plains to the rugged bays of the Banks Peninsula, the region offers a lot of interesting sights.

Ferrymead Heritage Park
This historic park about 15 minutes south of the centre re-creates the atmosphere of Christchurch in the early 20th century, with its old wooden houses, its church, school, railway station and prison. Old electric trams rattle along the roads at weekends and

during school holidays, and a vintage steam train runs on Sundays in December and January.

Port Hills

South of Christchurch rise the Port Hills. Summit Road Drive, along the crest of the hills, affords a splendid view of the Canterbury Plains and the Southern Alps to the west and Lyttelton Harbour 11 km (7 miles) to the southeast. This natural deep-water anchorage is the main port of the South Island. Three roadhouses stand along the route. The most interesting of them, the **Sign of the Takahe** (closed until spring 2013) resembles a Tudor manor, complete with carvings, coats of arms and heraldic shields. It was built in 1918. Alternatively, you can take the Gondola cable car from Heathcote Valley up to the top of the 448-m (1,470-ft) Mt Cavendish, from where the views are magnificent.

Banks Peninsula

From **Lyttelton**, a trading port overlooked by steep slopes covered with Victorian-era houses, the coast bulges out as the magnificent Banks Peninsula. It was created by two volcanoes, whose craters, submerged by the ocean, protect the ports of Lyttelton and Akaroa. It was sighted in 1770 by Captain Cook, who named it in honour of his shipboard col-

Crossing the Backbone.
Considered by connoisseurs to be one of the ten best train rides in the world, the **TranzAlpine Express** takes just over four hours to link the east and west coasts. Leaving Christchurch, the daily train traverses the Canterbury Plains, follows the **Waimakariri Gorge** through a series of tunnels and viaducts, to reach **Arthur's Pass Village** in the heart of the Southern Alps. After a stop it continues beneath the mountains to Otira railway village, before finally descending to Greymouth.

league, the naturalist Sir Joseph Banks.

In 1840, 57 French settlers and a few Germans, drawn by the whaling possibilities, decided to stay in **Akaroa**. Street and house names evoke these origins, the French flag flies over many of the shops, and descendants of the settlers still live in the pretty, flower-bedecked town. Its museum tells their story, and that of Frank Worsley (1872–1943), the heroic captain of the *Endurance* during Shackleton's unsuccessful expedition to the Antarctic.

Boat trips take visitors to see rare Hector dolphins, the smallest in the world. It is even possible to swim among them.

Orana Wildlife Park

Approximately 25 minutes by car northwest of the city centre, this is New Zealand's only open range zoo and also acts as a major centre of wildlife conservation. It specializes mainly in southern hemisphere wildlife from Africa, South America and Australasia, and encourages as much contact between visitors and animals as possible. You can hand-feed a giraffe, stroke a llama and get as close as you'd probably ever want to be to a pride of lions, thanks to the fact that here the visitors are in cages mounted on a car, while the lions roam free in their enormous enclosure. The zoo also has an excellent collection of rare New Zealand creatures on display, such as the kiwi, tuatara and kea, the world's only species of alpine parrot.

Lake Tekapo

Head inland from Geraldine to this popular tourist destination, with several resort hotels at the southern end. On the lake shores, the **Church of the Good Shepherd** (1935) is a favourite with photographers because its altar window provides a splendid frame for a mountain view.

Waitaki Valley

Further down the coast, the valley has a number of sights: **Duntroon**, named after a Scottish castle, has

istockphoto.com/McKie

A waterfall near Arthur's Pass in the middle of the South Island.

an authentic smithy, and you can go trout- or salmon fishing, or jet-boating. Hundreds of years ago, Maori artists left drawings in ochre and charcoal on the chalk cliffs of **Takiroa**. At the head of the valley, **Omarama** is famous for gliding thanks to its northwest currents and a fine view over the Southern Alps on a clear day.

Oamaru

A paradise for penguin-lovers, the port has a small colony of rare yellow-eyed penguins at Bushy Beach, where they return from

The boulders at Moeraki are known as the Devil's Marbles.

istockphoto.com/McKie

The West
The west coast is known for its wet weather; the clouds come from the west, cling to the mountains and rain down over the land. But it is specially famous for delicious whitebait, fried to a crisp, and for its precious greenstone, much prized by the Maoris. And for the pesky sandflies.

Punakaiki
The main attraction of this place is just by the highway: the spectacular **Pancake Rocks**, created by the action of the waves and particularly photogenic at sunrise or sunset. When the sea is rough, the water shoots through blowholes and cascades down the cliffs. Trips of one or several days are organized from here to the rainforest of **Paparoa National Park**.

Lake Brunner
Inland from **Greymouth**, the largest town on the west coast with something of a gold town atmosphere, the lake is a favourite with fishermen. Guides can be hired at Lake Brunner Lodge. The nearby **Moana Reserve** has a wildlife park where you can view indigenous species in natural surroundings.

Westland National Park
The **Fox Glacier** and **Franz Josef Glacier** are the stars of this park, presenting the unusual spectacle of vast walls of blue ice advancing

fishing every day about 2 hours before dusk. A larger colony of around 600 small blue penguins can be seen near an old quarry at the edge of the harbour. They come back home at nightfall.

Moeraki
The long beach 35 km (22 miles) south of Oamaru is famous for its large round rocks scattered over the sand. They were formed 60 to 65 million years ago and still fall down from the cliffs. A short way further south, **Shag Point** is home to a big colony of sea lions.

down close to the sea and into subtropical bushland. Or rather, not so much advancing as charging full steam ahead. Franz Josef moves at the rate of about 70 cm a day, and Fox about 1 m, though they have been known to speed up to 4 m (13 ft) daily. Franz Josef's icefall feeding into the Waiho River is an extraordinary sight. Guided walks are available to either of the glaciers, complete with boots and other necessary equipment and there are spectacular heli-hikes. Buses connect from Queenstown or Greymouth.

The Visitors Centre at each glacier can steer you to other walks in this marvellous park, perhaps taking you past Peter's Pool or Lake Wombat, kettleholes formed by melted glacial ice. In fine weather, Aoraki/Mt Cook is reflected in the waters of Lake Matheson near Fox.

Aoraki/Mt Cook National Park
The country's highest mountain rises to 3,754 m (12,317 ft). Surrounding it are 19 peaks reaching more than 3,080 m (10,000 ft). The Maori name for the monarch of the Southern Alps, officially recognized, means Cloud Piercer. It was first scaled on Christmas Day, 1894. Since then, many famous mountaineers have put themselves to the test in the area, including Sir Edmund Hillary, conqueror of Mt Everest and a New Zealander himself. The tip fell away in 1991, reducing the mountain's height by 10 m (33 ft).

Debris from the mountain slid as far as the Tasman Glacier. More than anything, it was glacial ice that sculpted the contours of the Southern Alps. Tasman, 27 km (17 miles) in length, up to 3 km (2 miles) wide, is the most famous of all the glaciers (among the longest in the world outside the polar regions). One of its subsidiaries, the Hochstetter, ends in a descent so tortuous it is known as an icefall.

Wildlife flourishes, despite the harsh climate. Tahr, chamois, red deer and hare were introduced into the area, but they all damage the environment. Among birds, you'll see the rock wren, the tiny rifleman, the New Zealand pigeon and the kea *(Nestor notabilis)*, a parrot that seems a uniform drab green until it reveals brilliant scarlet under its wings. At night you'll hear moreporks (the native owl) calling.

The subtle beauty of the alpine flowers is equally enthralling. One of the most attractive, the white-petalled mountain buttercup or Mount Cook lily, blooms from November to January.

Further south, **Mount Aspiring National Park** is one of the biggest and least developed of the country, dominated by the icy peak culminating at 3,033 m (9,950 ft).

hemis.fr/Gardel

Taking the plunge.

New Zealanders have a remarkable taste for extreme sports and adventure activities. Nothing exemplifies this more than AJ Hackett's role in making bungy jumping famous following his leap from the Eiffel Tower in 1987, a latex rubber cord attached to his ankle. Hackett returned to his homeland to establish the world's first commercial bungy jumping centre at the Kawarau Suspension Bridge just outside Queenstown on South Island. Today, Kawerau has a bungy museum and theatre, while more operations are to be found across the country and newer forms such as parabungy (jumping with a parachute) have made their appearance. Hackett was inspired by the Pentecost Islanders (Vanuatu) who since time immemorial have tested their manhood and ensured a good yam harvest by jumping from heights, attached to specially selected vines.

The South

The southern part of South Island is where New Zealand's landscape becomes truly dramatic. Fiordland is part of the southwest zone Te Wahipounamu, which includes Westland, Aoraki/Mt Cook and Mount Aspiring national parks and features on UNESCO's World Heritage list. Queenstown, meanwhile, is a centre of adrenaline-rush extreme sports such as bungy jumping and jet-boating. After all this, the restrained neo-classical Scottish cities of Dunedin and Invercargill will come as a welcome chance to slow down the pace for a while and enjoy the cultural pleasures of some of New Zealand's finest museums and art galleries.

Beyond lies Stewart Island, New Zealand's third-largest island and a practically unspoiled haven of peace and solitude.

Fiordland

Gateway to the country's largest national park is Te Anau, a small town living from tourism and raising deer. Up above the township in a small wildlife park live the last of the takahe, flightless birds with brilliant indigo and viridian plumage and rounded reddish bills. They were believed to be extinct, until they reappeared in 1948. Strangely, the very day they were found, a new cave was discovered in the area,

Te Anau-au. This is the only "living" cave in New Zealand, still being carved by the waters of the lake. A pleasant boat trip from the town takes you to an underground waterfall inside the cave and to a chamber lit by huge glow-worms.

There are scenic flights from Te Anau, and many trails in the area, including the four-day **Milford Track**, the "finest walk in the world" as it's proclaimed locally, which starts at the head of Lake Te Anau and ends at Milford Sound. Book several months ahead, as the number of hikers is strictly limited. But don't count on fine weather; it rains here 300 days a year.

Milford Sound

Whether you see it from sea level or a "flightseeing" plane, the majesty of Milford Sound will overwhelm you. Geologically, it's an ancient glacial trough invaded by a tentacle of the sea. Scenically, it's among the most sublime thrills of the Fiordland. You may well see Milford Sound in the rain—over 6,000 mm (240 in) per annum. But the heavy showers don't detract from the magnificence of the place, for the drops glisten on the forest trees, lend an ethereal glow to the mosses and set a thousand waterfalls leaping from the mountainsides reflected in the fiord. On a good day the

flickr.com/anoldent

Spectacular falls amid lush greenery, to be seen if you follow the Milford Track.

surface of the sound is as smooth as polished greenstone.

Boat and kayak tours of Milford Sound will bring you to the foot of the pyramid-shaped **Mitre Peak**, and close to **Bowen Falls** and the misty 150-m (500-ft) drop of **Stirling Falls** and sheer mountains where the trees are so closely matted in the thin soil that they actually provoke "bush avalanches". You'll see seals locking their flippers to float on the surface or sunbathing on warm grandstand rocks, while dolphins do a special turn around the boat. Of all the places you visit, this isolated ice-carved paradise may provide the memory that lasts the longest. A prosaic footnote: be sure to have some insect repellent at the ready. This is savage sand-fly country.

Doubtful Sound

From Te Anau, it is easy to reach the superb **Lake Manapouri**, 22 km (13 miles) to the south on the Invercargill road. A track from the lake winds up to Wilmot Pass then descends to the extraordinary fjord of Doubtful Sound, home to bottlenose dolphins and rare Fiordland crested penguins. You can also get there by boat.

Queenstown

This cheerful resort town in sight of the rugged Remarkables mountain range and with a lovely setting in a bay on the shores of Lake Wakatipu has managed to carve out a name for itself as the adventure capital of the world— it was here that A.J. Hackett commercialized bungy jumping. There are several jumps at 43 m (141 ft), 71 m (233 ft) or 102 m (335 ft), plunging into the river, if you so wish. The most popular is **Kawarau Bridge** (the lowest of the three). If that seems tame, take a "Big Jump" from a helicopter, which will throw you overboard at 300 m (1,000 ft).

Try the Kawarau or the Shotover River jet-boating experience and you'll be talking about it for the rest of your life. Almost as nerve-tingling are the river raft trips, white-water sledging and river surfing. There's the extra bonus of top-class skiing at Coronet Peak and a little further away at Cardrona, to keep the adrenaline levels high in winter as well as summer. There are several good freeride mountain biking tracks, and you can go heli-skiing.

The **Skyline Gondola**, one of the steepest lifts anywhere, skims from the centre up Bob's Peak for a view over the town, the lake and the mountains. There's a restaurant at the top, as well as a bungy jump platform.

At the foot of the Gondola, the **Kiwi and Birdlife Park** has a nocturnal house for the kiwis and other rare endemic birds.

Wander the streets of the small town centre, and along the lake promenade, to the vast **Queenstown Gardens**. Set on a peninsula jutting into the lake, they boast secular trees and an enormous boulder commemorating Antarctic explorer Robert Falcon Scott.

Lake Wakatipu

The name means "Where the Demon Lies". The legend has it that the demon's heart is still beating at the bottom of the lake, which explains the strange pulsating of the waters—its level varies by 12 cm (5 in) every 5 minutes!

The grand old lady of the lake is the *Earnslaw*, a coal-burning steamer, built in Dunedin in 1912. It is now used for short cruises combined with various activities such as picnics and horse riding. You may prefer a less colourful but faster launch to one of the big sheep stations such as **Walter Peak**, where the sheepdogs round up the flocks. You can fish the lake for rainbow and brown trout and quinnat salmon.

Glenorchy

A scenic drive brings you here in an hour from Queenstown, along the shores of Lake Wakatipu. From Glenorchy, take the gravel road to **Paradise**, whose road sign, Paradise—No Exit, is the most photographed in the country. The landscape, with white-capped mountains and clear blue river, is so extraordinary that it comes as no surprise to learn that it was chosen for the site of Lothlorien, land of the elves, in *The Lord of the Rings*. Some of the best alpine hikes start out from here; Routeburn, Caples and Greenstone tracks; day trips are available.

Arrowtown

A short drive from Queenstown, the mining village of Arrowtown, with a few Chinese buildings,

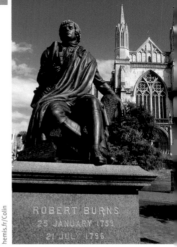

hemis.fr/Colin

Dunedin honours Robbie Burns because one of the founders was his nephew; the poet's statue was funded by the local Burns Club.

recreates the atmosphere of the roaring 1860s. You can try your hand at panning here or at nearby Goldfields.

Dunedin

If Christchurch can be described as "the most English city outside England", Dunedin in a deep bay the southeast coast might make the same sort of claim for its kindred Scottish spirit. This a second Edinburgh of imposing stone buildings, soaring spires, and culture—you might detect a Scottish burr in the speech patterns. With a population of 124,000, Dunedin is the home of the country's oldest university.

The Octagon
Right in the municipal bull's-eye, the Octagon is a spacious square appropriately embellished with a statue of Robert Burns. The Scots poet is seated with "his back to the kirk and his face to the pub". Actually the kirk in question, the Gothic Revival **St Paul's Cathedral**, outlived the pub, which has been demolished. Burns also chooses to turn his back to the **Municipal Chambers** dating from 1880, and of Italian Renaissance inspiration.

Dunedin Public Art Gallery
Located on the southwest corner of the Octagon, the museum displays works by New Zealand's world-famous painter, Frances Hodgkins, who was born in Dunedin. Also represented are works by modern artists, alongside European paintings from the Renaissance to the 20th century.

Stuart Street
Bisecting the Octagon, this street leads down to the **Law Courts** and the marvellously exuberant **railway station**, completed in 1906 with a mosaic floor of Minton tiles and stained-glass windows depicting a steam train.

The nearby **Otago Settlers Museum** has a collection of pioneer and gold rush mementoes, and a section devoted to means of transport, with a splendid steam engine dating from 1872.

Otago Museum
The museum, 1 km north of the Octagon on Great King Street, houses an outstanding collection of Maori, Melanesian and other Pacific Island material, including a superb war canoe. There's also an intriguing natural history section and Discovery World, an interactive science museum that's sure to entertain the children.

Olveston House
A five-minute walk west of the Otago Museum is this gracious Edwardian residence, built between 1904 and 1906 in Jacobean style for the wealthy Theomin family. The interior is especially impressive, and is richly furnished with European and Asian furniture and antiques and early New Zealand paintings.

Otago Peninsula
Jutting out north of Dunedin, the peninsula is endowed with fantastic wildlife. **Taiaroa Head** is the only mainland place in the world where you can see a royal albatross colony. Clumsy when on land, these enormous birds are impressively graceful in flight,

usually at day's end when the wind picks up. The rare hoiho or yellow-eyed penguin (its head is yellow too) and Hooker's sea lion also inhabit the peninsula, which has beautiful beaches and dunes.

The Catlins

Between Dunedin and Invercargill, the Catlins resemble the Scottish highlands. The area is a living museum, rich in flora and fauna found nowhere else in the world: trees bent by the winds, yellow-eyed penguins and fur seals, especially at **Nugget Point**. At **Curio Bay** there's a fossil forest, visible only at low tide.

Invercargill

New Zealand's southernmost city shares Dunedin's Scottish background. Well-planned and conservative, Invercargill draws its wealth from food processing and agriculture.

Southland Museum and Art Gallery

This large museum is close to the entrance to Queen's Park on Victoria Avenue. There are displays on local Maori tribes, Victorian Invercargill, New Zealand's sub-Antarctic islands and the remarkable tuatara, a type of lizard only found in this corner of the globe. The art gallery puts on temporary exhibitions of foreign and New Zealand artists.

Stewart Island

The trade and fishing port of **Bluff**, 27 km (17 miles) to the south of Invercargill, is known throughout the country for its oysters. It is also the departure point for ferries to Stewart Island 30 km (18 miles) across the Foveaux Strait.

Most of the island's 500 inhabitants live in **Oban**, a friendly fishing village and the only settlement, on the north coast. Find out more about its history at the Rakiura Museum.

There are hardly any roads in this haven of beach and forest — 85 per cent of the island is protected from development as the **Rakiura National Park**. You can scout the northern area, but the south, facing the Antarctic, is almost unexplored. Be out and about at sunrise or sunset to see the spectacular colours. It's possible to see the *aurora australis*, or southern lights, from here. This probably explains the Maori name for the island: Rakiura literally means "glowing skies".

Should Stewart Island prove too crowded, take the 10-minute boat trip to the tiny **Ulva Island** in the Paterson Inlet. With sandy beaches and a great variety of ferns and orchids, it's a protected area for birds such as the tui, kakariki (red-crowned parakeet), dotterel, weka, kaka, kiwi, kereru pigeon and the tiny jade-green titipounamou.

CUSTOMS AND CULTURE

Haka

The word *haka* is a generic Maori term for dance by men or women, but it has become associated specifically with the extraordinary warrior dance intended to highlight the fighting man's power and scare his enemies stiff. The version devised by Te Rauparaha, a chief of the Ngati Toa tribe in the early 19th century, has become famous around the world thanks to the All Blacks rugby team.

The *haka* they perform before kick-off involves energetic foot-pounding and thigh- and chest-slapping, along with enough thrusting out of tongues and bulging of eyes to intimidate the bravest opponents. The fierce chant that accompanies it uses the words of Te Rauparaha's:

ka mate ka mate
ka ora ka ora
(It is death, it is death
It is life, it is life)

So inextricably linked is the *haka* with New Zealand's success on the rugby field that when it was suggested by the team coach that the All Blacks stop performing it, the outcry was heard throughout the whole country.

Literature

The first unquestionably great New Zealand writer was Wellington-born **Katherine Mansfield** (1888–1923). Her mastery of the short story form was based upon a remarkable ability to evoke the drama of her characters' psychological states through a subtle, poetic prose style. Although she spent most of her adult life in Europe, her best stories such as *Prelude, At the Bay* and *The Voyage* are set in New Zealand and revolve around Mansfield's memories of her childhood there.

The short stories of **Frank Sargeson** (1903–82) employ a robust use of the vernacular and will challenge and engage the non-New Zealand reader. Sargeson is little known outside his homeland, but his finely tuned ear for authentic dialogue and keen eye for colourful characters mark him out as one of the country's finest writers. His stories were published in *Conversations with my Uncle, A Man and his Wife*, and *That Summer, and other stories*.

Janet Frame (1924–2004) wrote several novels that take for their subject a parochial society's inability to deal with madness, the irrational and individuals who don't fit in, something that reflected her own experience of life in New Zealand—she spent several years in mental hospitals. Frame is probably best known for her excellent three-volume autobiography *An Angel at My Table*, made into an award-winning film by director Jane Campion in 1990.

A surprise Booker Prize winner in 1985, **Keri Hulme**'s complex, mystical *The Bone People* is set in the South Island. Hulme (b. 1947) is of mixed Maori and British ancestry, and what has to date been her only novel focuses on both elements of New Zealand society.

Sir Edmund Hillary (1919–2008)

When Edmund Hillary and his Nepalese companion Tenzing Norgay became the first people to reach the summit of Mt Everest in 1953, they found instant worldwide fame. But how did an obscure one-time bee-keeper from the country town-ship of Tuakau, 64 km (40 miles) south of Auckland, manage to turn into the man who conquered the high-est place on

earth? It all began with a school trip to Mt Ruapehu in the centre of North Island in the winter of 1935. What he found there changed his life. He recounts in his autobiography *View from the Summit* how this was "the most exciting thing that had ever happened to me at that time and undoubtedly the start of my enthusiasm for snow and mountains." He was later able to cut his mountaineering teeth on the great Southern Alps of the South Island. After serving as a navigator in the Royal New Zealand Air Force during World War II and then running a bee-keeping farm with his brother, Hillary prepared for the great Everest expedition by tackling New Zealand's own mighty Aoraki/Mt Cook. In 1948 he and three colleagues were the first ever to climb its South Ridge. Success paved the way for greater things five years later. But Sir Edmund's explanation of how he became a world-famous mountaineer is simple and still rings true today: "adventure is always near at hand in New Zealand."

If you like seafood, you can dine like royalty at a seaside shack.

OPEN
LOBSTER

W tartare

HOT !
CRAYFISH
W garlic

OR

MUSSELS

DINING OUT

Until relatively recently, New Zealand's approach to food was mainly influenced by the population's British origins and followed the "lamb and two veg" school of cooking. But the 21st century has arrived with a culinary bang. While meat still dominates the menu, the range of different types of meat and styles of cooking now on offer is striking.

This is due in part to the influx of people—and their culinary traditions—from countries around the Mediterranean, Asia and the Pacific Rim. But it also reflects an increasing awareness among the nation's chefs of the sheer variety and quality of home-grown ingredients, from fish and shellfish to amazingly fresh fruits and tasty herbs. On top of all this, New Zealand's wine makers have surpassed themselves in coming up with superb wines ranging from rich chocolatey pinot noirs to fruity chardonnays, a match for any from the best vineyards in the world.

To Start With...

Locals tend to favour lighter breakfasts consisting of fruit, cereal, yoghurt, juice and coffee. But they haven't completely shaken off their British roots and if you stay at a Bed & Breakfast you'll probably get a "full English": large quantities of eggs, bacon, sausages, toast that will be certain to keep you going on the busiest day's sightseeing.

Fish and Seafood

For tasty seafood in a hurry, you can find takeaway deep-fried oysters and mussels, and *paua* (abalone) fritters. If this seems a tad too exotic, there's always the tried and tested delight of fresh fish and chips (or *fush and chups* as they pronounce it in these parts), wrapped in paper.

On a more elegant plane, try the crayfish (spiny lobster), scallops, and fish as flavourful as snapper, grouper (frequently referred to by its Maori name, *hapuku*) and John Dory. Blue cod comes from the Chatham Islands and succulent Bluff oysters are fished from the cold, clean waters off the southernmost part of

South Island, while the superb green-lipped mussel hails from Marlborough Sound (the green lip is around the edge of the shell). *Toheroa* is an exceptionally large—and expensive—clam harvested on Ninety Mile Beach.

You'll find plenty of lobster, shrimp and prawn on the menu, while salmon, both smoked and fresh, can be found everywhere. Look out for seafood with a zingy Pacific Rim twist in dishes such as Cantonese steamed New Zealand snapper and char-grilled prawns in miso.

Tasty seafood pâtés made from crayfish or smoked eel can be excellent, as is the popular "raw" fish starter made from *tarakihi*, a firm-fleshed, delicately flavoured saltwater fish marinated in lemon juice until it turns opaque, served with coconut milk.

Meat

On most menus meat dishes will feature lamb in some form or other. The traditional meal of roasted home-reared, grass-fed lamb or hogget (the name given to sheep from 12 to 18 months old) as chops served with mint sauce might almost be a culinary cliché in New Zealand, but it's still delicious due to the quality of the meat. Adventurous *nouvelle* variations influenced by overseas cuisine abound in the smarter restaurants of Auckland and Wel-lington, accompanied by local vegetables such as *kumara*, a type of sweet potato, silver beet, resembling Swiss chard, and *kumi-kumi*, a local variety of pumpkin. The so-called Colonial Goose is actually a roast leg of lamb stuffed with dried apricots and honey. Game such as boar and venison, or quail, duck and pheasant, are mouthwateringly served with mountain berries.

In summer, outdoor barbecues are very popular, and feature beef, lamb and seafood. A special treat for tourists in the North Island is the *hangi* (pronounced hung-ee), a Maori feast of meats, seafood and vegetables such as kumara (sweet potatoes) prepared in an *umu*, or earth oven, a pit lined with red-hot stones and covered with leaves. Traditionally, the men dig out the hole and the women prepare the food.

The venerable New Zealand meat pie can be bought at bakeries and bars and makes for a tasty lunchtime snack.

Desserts

Cheese-making is a growing industry in New Zealand and you will discover many good handmade cheeses, especially from ewe's or goat's milk.

For the most refreshing sweet desserts, look for local fruits like apples, grapes, cherries, passion-fruit, oranges, tangelos, feijoas and kiwi fruit. The calorific option is Pavlova, a meringue disk topped with fresh fruit and whipped cream. An old favourite, hokey-pokey ice cream combines vanilla ice cream and golden caramel chunks.

Drinks

Fine New Zealand wines are available everywhere. In North Island, main growing areas are around Auckland, Hawke's Bay, Gisborne and Martinborough. In South Island, around Marlborough, Blenheim, Canterbury and Queenstown areas. Most restaurants are fully licensed. If not, they are signposted BYO, which means you can bring your own bottle. Local beer is very good and reasonably priced. Especially worth sampling are the beers produced by microbreweries, such as the organic Founders Brewery in Nelson and the award-winning Aotearoa Breweries in the East Cape region. *Titoki* liqueur is distilled from berries and a shrub.

Something of a coffee culture has sprung up, as proved by the abundance of many excellent coffee shops. A Flat White is a strong latte, a Short Black an espresso.

The Chinese gooseberry was renamed kiwi fruit by New Zealand exporters in the 1950s. | What do you fancy: lamb chops, green-lipped mussels or a pie?

At the Maori model village near Rotorua you can watch woodcarvers at work.

Guy Minder

SHOPPING

New Zealand's fine craftwork items embrace both Maori and European traditions, while clothing made from sheepskin and leather will give you warm memories of your visit through the long winter days back at home. All are available in the shops and boutiques of Auckland and Wellington, but if you're travelling around the country you should wait to see whether the range and price on offer is more advantageous in the place of production.

Where to Shop

Fashion design is a fast-growing creative industry in New Zealand. Head to places like Cuba Street in Wellington, High Street, Ponsonby Road and Parnell in Auckland and along Christchurch's High Street for the trendiest designer clothes. For something more traditional try Wellington's upmarket department store Kirkcaldie & Stains on Lambton Quay. The Saturday Otara Market in Manukau near Auckland, is a great place to find clothes, crafts, food and music from around the South Pacific. Held on Sundays, the Avondale market draws up to 15,000 visitors. The Maori Arts and Crafts Institute in Whakarewarewa at Rotorua sells exquisite if expensive examples of Maori art. Greenstone items can be found in Hokitika's craft shops.

Clothing

It will come as no surprise to find that New Zealand is a leading manufacturer of sheepskin and wool products. You'll see so many luxurious sheepskin rugs and mats that it's hard to resist buying one. A pair of cosy sheepskin slippers wll keep your toes toasty at night.

Other good choices are fleece-lined suede jackets and multi-coloured sweaters and scarves,, while woollen gloves, hats and lamb'swool muffs are also sure to please. Merino wool is sometimes mixed with 30 per cent possum fur for added softness.

Genuine ugg boots, the internationally trendy sheepskin gumboots, are manufactured in New Zealand and available at high street retailers in all the main cities.

Handicrafts

There's a long-standing crafts tradition from within New Zealand's European population. Craftsmen fashion local timber into a variety of wooden articles: bowls, plates, goblets, trays, bookends and—for children—attractive chunky toys, puzzles, inlaid rulers and pencil-boxes. Other items, such as vases, are made out of *ponga* (fernwood). You'll also find household goods, jewellery and numerous other items fashioned from materials such as ceramic, glass and silk.

Maori Craftwork

Top-quality Maori carvings can be expensive. Look out for beautiful *whakairo rakau*, highly decorative woodcarvings depicting mythical forms, indigenous animals and so on, along with carved boxes, masks and imitation war canoes. Maori art has now been turned to all aspects of the souvenir market, and you will also be able to find decorated tablemats, napkins, ashtrays, earrings, T-shirts and carrier bags. Gourds incised with Maori motifs make attractive containers for dried flowers, or unusual wine and water decanters.

Greenstone—local jade or nephrite and known as *pounamu* in Maori—ranges in colour from pale to dark green. You'll find it carved into tasteful pendants called *paonga* (which, traditionally, you should buy only as a gift, not for yourself), bracelets, cufflinks, rings and handles of cutlery. The main motifs for pendants are miniature *tikis*, ritual fertility or protective symbols with their tongues sticking out in the Maori sign of challenge. Hei-Tiki was the first man, who came from the stars. They are also made in the shape of fish hooks, which symbolize prosperity and good health, the spiral *koru*, representing new beginnings, growth and harmony, *mere* (clubs), ensuring triumph over adversity, and *pikorua* or infinity, a symbol of the strength and beauty of enduring friendship and two interwoven lives.

Similar items are made from semi-precious stones and bone. In a silver setting, small pieces of abalone shell (*paua*) make attractive jewellery; they are also sold whole in the form of practical items such as dishes or ashtrays. Note that it is illegal to take *paua* shells that haven't been turned into ornaments out of New Zealand.

Other Items

Perfumes based on the essence of native flowers make attractive gifts, as do liqueurs made from subtropical fruits or shrubs. The strong-flavoured *manuka* or tea tree honey is renowned for its healing properties, and in the cosmetics department you'll find numerous products based on the products of the bee—propolis, beeswax and royal jelly in various face creams and other preparations.

New Zealand's wines, especially those from vineyards around Hawke's Bay and Marlborough, can easily compete with the finest in the world. There are dozens of different vineyards you can visit in these regions that offer tastings, so you should be able to find exactly the type that suits your palate.

Given New Zealanders' passion for enjoying the great outdoors, it should be no wonder that some of the world's best hiking equipment is from here. Camping gear such as tents and sleeping bags, weather-proof jackets and rucksacks are made by firms like the renowned Macpac.

Somewhat less specialized are the souvenir goods which play on the country's classic icons. Items as diverse as All Black rugby shirts and jerseys, carved kakapo parrot decorations, kiwi T-shirts and kiwi fruit chocolates make memorable and inexpensive gifts.

istockphoto.com/Tuftnell

istockphoto.com/Neish

Barbara Ender-Jones

An out-thrust tongue provides protection from evil forces. | Greenstone spiral, or *koru*, pendant. | The pukeko gets everywhere, even onto socks.

Even before a friendly match, the All Blacks
try to intimidate the opposing team.

SPORTS

Most New Zealanders are sports mad. When they're not making the most of their fantastic landscape, be it skiing in the mountains, surfing off the coast or simply tramping (hiking) through the Great Outdoors, they're likely to be following the latest exploits on the field of the All Blacks rugby team or their national cricket side. Visitors will find it hard to avoid joining in the action.

Water Sports

You can go swimming at any of the beautiful beaches around the country, though you'll need to make sure that you choose a spot where the powerful surf isn't a danger. Stick to areas monitored by lifeguards. The opportunities for scuba diving and snorkelling in crystal clear waters shouldn't be missed—though even in high summer the sea is quite cold.

The challenging nature of the surf makes New Zealand a surfer's paradise. Raglan is internationally renowned for its stunning left-handed break, while the Taranaki coast can boast the superlative "Surf Highway", with kilometres of world-class surf beaches such as Fitzroy, Oakura and Stent Road. Windsurfers profit from the lively nautical conditions around the coast between October and February. Popular spots are Auckland harbour, the Hauraki Gulf and Wellington (at Plimmerton and Lyall Bay), where you'll be able to rent boards and other equipment without too much difficulty.

Sea- and river-kayaking are both possible, along with some fearsome white-water rafting between October and May in the fast-flowing rivers of both the main islands.

Anglers will love the first-rate salmon fishing in the rivers of the South Island, especially around Otago. North Island is known more for its trout fishing. The thrill of big-game fishing can be enjoyed around the top end of the North Island, with shark, tuna and marlin being the main targets.

On Land

Tramping (hiking) usually involves at least a three-day walk through the spectacular scenery of one of the great national parks.

It's an extremely popular pursuit among New Zealanders, allowing them to commune with the natural wonders of their country. In a similar vein, you can also go horse trekking and mountain biking, and get to grips with the landscape through caving, rock climbing and mountaineering.

Winter Sports

New Zealand's ski and snowboarding season runs from mid June to early October. You can take your pick from downhill, cross-country, ski mountaineering and, for daring skiers with healthy bank balances, heli-skiing in the Southern Alps, where you are dropped by helicopter at inaccessible spots in the mountains and ski down virgin slopes.

Skiing in New Zealand is generally a pretty laid-back affair and there are few large resorts in the European or American style. The best North Island skiing can be found on the volcanic Mt Ruapehu, with its resorts of Whakapapa, Turoa and Tukino. But without doubt the main place for skiing is the South Island, with the Southern Alps providing a wide range of skiing areas centred on resorts such as Queenstown, Wanaka, Christchurch and Mackenzie.

Extreme Sports

While bungy jumping—leaping off high bridges and platforms with a rubber cord around your legs to stop you hitting the ground —wasn't invented in New Zealand, it was first developed here as an organized activity. It's not for the faint-hearted, but for those who crave the adrenaline rush of a truly extreme sport, it can't be beaten. There are plenty of other sports available here that try, however. Skydiving, pot-holing, canyoning, rafting or river sledging will all test the limits of your nerve.Tandem flights, with the

Hike a trail. The **Abel Tasman Coastal Track** passes through the golden beaches of Tasman Bay and fine native bushland. The **Tongariro Crossing** is a marvellous one-day hike across lava flows, around craters and through virgin bush, with sensational views of the Tongariro National Park's three huge volcanoes. **Milford Track**, in the South Island's fiord country, is one of the most famous in the world, with 51 km (32 miles) of breathtaking scenery. The short trail to **Kea Point** offers great opportunities to appreciate Aoraki/Mt Cook, New Zealand's highest mountain. The **Rakiura Track**, on Stewart Island, takes you on a circuit around part of the island, with its fascinating plant and bird life.

reassurance of being attached to a qualified instructor, will get you a similar thrill. And why not try zorbing—strapped into a large plastic, air-cushioned ball, you roll downhill in a state that's close to weightlessness.

Spectator Sports

The national sport is rugby union, and the All Blacks are always expected to win. The country hosted the first World Cup in 1987 and again in 2011, when they confirmed their rank with a victory over France in the final. The All Blacks compete in the annual SupeRugby 14 competition from end February to early August, where they are pitted against the Australia and South Africa. The national ITM Cup, whose season begins end July and ends in early November, is equally popular with New Zealanders.

Cricket takes over sports fans' interest in the summer months, with a provincial league held from November to March and the national side, the Blackcaps, involved in international matches (called test matches) at the main stadiums around the country.

istockphoto.com/Bousquet

istockphoto.com/Spedding

istockphoto.com/Shiffman

Looking out from the top of the antipodean world. | There are good surfing beaches all around the two main islands. | The thrills of white-water rafting near Rotorua.

Don't start counting them or you'll fall asleep at the wheel.

hemis.fr/Gardel

THE HARD FACTS

To help you plan your trip, here are some of the practical details you should know about New Zealand.

Airports

The main international gateways to New Zealand are Auckland, Wellington and Christchurch.

Auckland International Airport is located 20 km (12 miles) south of the city centre. There's a free shuttle bus between terminals, and free showers if you need to freshen up after a long flight. The AirBus service leaves every 10 minutes from 6 a.m. to 7 p.m. and every 20–30 minutes in the evening for the city centre, while the more expensive Supershuttle offers a door-to-door service.

Wellington International Airport is just 8 km (5 miles) southeast of the city. You can take a Supershuttle minibus to your hotel from outside its only terminal, though the regular Stagecoach Airport Flyer service to the city centre is a far cheaper option.

Christchurch Airport is the South Island's main international airport. It's 10 km (6 miles) northwest of the city and has a freephone service for hotel and car hire bookings. It also has Super Shuttle minibuses for door-to-door delivery at your hotel. Again, the local CityFlyerBus service to the centre of Christchurch costs considerably less.

All of these airports have excellent foreign exchange, ATM and baggage storage facilities, as well as visitor centres providing information and hotel booking services. Taxis are always available (though note there is a surcharge after 10 p.m.).

Climate

New Zealand's seasons are the opposite of those in Europe, which means that the high season when tourist attractions and beaches are at their busiest is during the months from December to February, while the best skiing and snowboarding is to be had from June and October. The weather is very changeable; you can sometimes experience four seasons in one day.

There are distinct differences in climate between the two main islands. North Island is subtropical and has no extremes of heat or cold, while winter in the temperate South Island can be cool with snow falling in the mountains.

Lightweight cottons can be worn year-round in the North Island and in summer in the South Islands; it's best to wear several layers so you can remove or add them when required. Medium-weight clothes are necessary for the winter months in the south. A raincoat will prove essential everywhere and is especially necessary for visits to the rainforests in the South Island. Even in the cities dress tends to be casual.

Communications

New Zealand's postal service is efficient. Post offices are now generally known as "post shops", as they mostly occupy modern shop spaces rather than the great Victorian post office buildings of old. They offer a poste restante service and also sell stamps and phonecards.

Public telephones function with a Telecom PhoneCard or a credit card; some take coins, and some have a port for Internet access. You can also bring your own cellphone and buy a local SIM card and phone number for it, and then purchase prepaid cards. The main company offering this service is Vodafone, who have shops in most towns and cities, but another good and inexpensive one is 2degrees.

For directory assistance call 018, for international directory enquiries call 0172. To telephone abroad from New Zealand, dial 00 44 + the area code (minus the initial zero) + local number. The country code for dialling New Zealand from overseas is +64.

You'll find Internet Cafés in all but the smallest towns, and most hotels and hostels offer some form of online access, rarely free and limited in time as well as capacity. You will often find free access in public libraries.

Crime

New Zealand is a fairly safe place for travellers, though as in most countries it is wise to take precautions against theft, especially in the cities. Leave your valuables in the hotel safety deposit box where possible, beware of pickpockets in crowded places and always keep your money and passport well concealed, preferably in a money belt or sealable pocket. Make sure that cars are locked when unattended. Never leave bags or other objects that might look like they contain anything of value visible in a parked car.

Customs

Visitors over 17 years of age may import the following goods duty free: 200 cigarettes or 250 g of tobacco or 50 cigars or an assortment of these up to 250 g; three bottles max. 1,125 ml spirits; 4.5 litres of wine or beer, and other goods up to a value of $700. There are very strict regulations against potential sources of disease and pestilence: plants, animal products and foodstuffs of any kind are banned from being brought into the country. On-the-spot fines or refusal of entry can be the price for contravening these rules. If you are unsure about any goods you are carrying be sure to notify a customs officer. For more information visit:

www.customs.govt.nz

Driving

New Zealand might not be a big country in geographical terms, but its low population density and magnificent terrain can make much of it seem far from the madding crowd. For this reason, probably the best way to see the country beyond the cities is by car. All the main international car hire firms are represented here, while local ones are often cheaper. The advantage of using a major company is that they are more likely to offer the possibility of one-way rentals, though this can be a more expensive option. Overall, though, the number of companies in the market means that competition is fierce and prices reasonable. To rent a car, drivers must be over 21 years old and have a full, valid driving licence. Note that not all firms allow their cars to be taken across the Cook Strait, so check before you drive off.

Campervan hire is especially popular in New Zealand, and allows visitors to cut down on accommodation costs when they're on the road. Camping grounds where you can park up for the night are ubiquitous and generally have excellent facilities. Campervans are hired through specialized companies such as

Maui: www.maui.co.nz
Britz: www.britz.co.nz
Jucy: www.jucy.co.nz
Backpacker:
www.backpackervans.co.nz

The roads are good, well-sign-posted and usually uncrowded, and petrol is inexpensive by European standards.

Driving is on the left, as in the UK, but be aware that there is a "priority from the right" rule in New Zealand that's strictly adhered to by locals, so you'll need to give way to vehicles coming from the right at all times. Seatbelts are compulsory for all passengers.

There are countless single-lane bridges out in the countryside: priority is indicated by a sign before the bridge. You should also be prepared to encounter large flocks of sheep and slow-moving farm vehicles on the road at any time. Speed limits are 100 kph (62 mph) on open roads outside towns, 50 kph (31 mph) in built-up areas, unless otherwise indicated.

Electricity
230 volt, 50 Hz. Plugs have three flat angled pins, different from both British and Continental versions, so you will require an adaptor. Most hotels also have outlets for 110-volt electric razors.

Emergencies
In case of a serious emergency dial 111, free from any phone, to reach the police, fire brigade or ambulance service.

Entry formalities
Australian citizens can stay indefinitely in New Zealand, while British passport holders receive an automatic 6-month permit on arrival. Citizens of most other European countries, Japan, the USA and Canada are granted three-month permits, though it's fairly easy to get an extension if necessary. Those from other countries will need to obtain a visa prior to their arrival in New Zealand. If you are unsure about your status contact your nearest New Zealand consulate or visit the Immigration Service website:
www.immigration.govt.nz

Above all, make sure that your passport is valid for at least one month after the date that you plan to leave New Zealand.

Health
No vaccinations are required for entry into New Zealand. The nation's medical facilities are of a high standard, and citizens from countries such as the UK and Australia can obtain free emergency treatment under reciprocal healthcare agreements, while all visitors are covered to a limited extent under the accident compensation scheme. Given that you might find yourself in a remote corner of the country and would still need to pay for the transportation costs, it is wise to take out personal insurance for full emergency cover—including dangerous sports and activities if you intend to go skiing, surfing or bungy jumping, for example—before you leave home.

The fact is, however, that New Zealand is generally a healthy place to be and the greatest hazard will probably be too much exposure to the sun. Visitors from cooler climates need to take great care to protect themselves against the sun's intensity: you can be burnt to a crisp even on overcast days, so always wear a high-factor (30 or over) sun block, sunhat and sunglasses when outside, and be particularly careful between

11 a.m. and 3 p.m., when the sun is at its most powerful.

If you require specialized prescription medicines, take enough with you to last for the duration of your stay in case you have difficulties obtaining a supply when you are in New Zealand.

New Zealand has no poisonous creatures except for the very rare katipo spider, but on the South Island, sandflies, while not likely to give you any nasty diseases, can become a real nuisance if insect repellent is not used—the itching lasts for days.

Holidays

New Zealand's public holidays are as follows:

January 1–2	*New Year*
February 6	*Waitangi Day*
April 25	*Anzac Day*
June	*Queen's*
(1st Mon)	*Birthday*
October	*Labour Day*
(4th Mon)	
December 25	*Christmas Day*
December 26	*Boxing Day*

Moveable: Good Friday, Easter Monday

In addition to the above public holidays, each province also has its own anniversary day holiday commemorating the foundation of the provinces that were originally self-governing. These include:

Wellington	Jan 22
Auckland	Jan 29
Otago	March 23
Canterbury	Dec.16

In reality, the holiday is usually held on the closest Monday or Friday to these official dates, and celebrated with festivals of local culture.

Language

The two official languages are English and Maori. New Zealand English is spoken with a strong characteristic accent that, while similar to its Australian cousin, is most notable for its intriguingly mangled vowel sounds where, for example, "that" becomes "thet" and "fish" sounds like "fush". New Zealanders also tend to end every sentence with the interrogative "eh?" even if they haven't been asking a question. Maori is a Polynesian language spoken by about 150,000 of New Zealand's Maori population, all bilingual. Although the language was in danger of being lost through the dominance of English, it has undergone something of a revival among younger Maoris, and official documents and radio broadcasts are also produced in the language, while a Maori TV channel started broadcasting in 2004.

Money

The unit of currency is the New Zealand dollar (abbreviated to $ or NZ$), which is divided into 100 cents (c). Coins are issued in denominations of 10, 20 and 50c, $1 and $2; banknotes have values of $5, 10, 20, 50 and 100.

International credit cards are widely accepted at hotels, restaurants and shops, especially in the cities and popular tourist areas. Travellers cheques are not issued in NZ$; Australian, Canadian and US$ cheques are accepted, as well as those in Euros, pounds sterling and Japanese yen. You'll need to show your passport to confirm your identity when using them. Alternatively, if you have an international cashpoint card you can withdraw money from cash machines (ATMs) at banks such as Bank of New Zealand, ASB, Westpac and ANZ using your own PIN code. There are no banks or cash machines in Hauraki Gulf and on Stewart Island, where some shops only accept cash.

Opening hours

The following times are a general guide, and some of them may be subject to local variations.

Banks are open Monday to Friday 9 a.m.–4.30 p.m.; in towns some open on Saturday morning or even all weekend. Exchange bureaux usually open also on Saturdays and Sundays.

Post offices open Monday to Friday 8 or 9 a.m.–5 or 5.30 p.m. and on Saturday mornings in the main cities.

Shops are usually open on weekdays 9 a.m.–5 p.m. Many also open on Saturdays and some on Sundays, too, usually from 10 a.m. to 4 p.m. Shops keep longer hours in resort towns and large cities, where they will also often have late night shopping on either Thursday or Friday.

Public transport

Air. Internal flights around the country will be of particular use to those with limited amounts of time in the country. Air New Zealand offers links between all the main cities and towns, and Jetstar serves the main routes at reduced fares. Competition keeps the prices relatively low. There are also services to the remote Chatham Islands, Stewart Island and Great Barrier Island. If you're planning to do a lot of air travel you might consider buying an Air New Zealand air pass, available only to overseas residents.

Intercity Buses. An extensive network of buses reaches throughout the North and South Islands. The main operator is InterCity, which has a sister company called Newmans focused on luxury travel. They offer a Flexi-Pass, among others, valid for 12 months and with which you can buy travel at an hourly basis. There are several smaller operators, such as Atomic, that compete with InterCity and, if you're happy with less comfort, lower prices and lively fellow passengers, there are what's known as "backpacker buses", such as Kiwi Experience, Strav and Magic Bus.

Trains. Long-distance train travel is a fairly slow affair and most New Zealanders have given it up these days for motor or air transport. The journeys are still popular with tourists, which is unsurprising given that they run through some of the most spectacular scenery in the country. The 12-hour Overlander train goes from Auckland to Wellington and the Coastal Pacific runs from Christchurch via Kaikoura to Picton, while the TranzAlpine between Christchurch and Greymouth over Arthur's Pass is without question one of the world's greatest train rides.

These services are operated by Tranz Scenic:

www.tranzscenic.co.nz

tel. 0800 872 467

The 7- or 14-day Scenic Rail Pass is valid on these three segments, and also includes a ferry trip.

Ferries. If you want to see both of New Zealand's main islands, then, unless you fly, you'll have to take a boat across the Cook Strait. Bluebridge Ferries:

www.bluebridge.co.nz

and the Interislander:

www.interislandline.co.nz

cover the distance between Wellington and Picton in around 3 hours, while Interislander's fast Lynk catamaran does it in just over 2 hours. Try to book as far in advance as possible for discount fares. Stewart Island is connected to the mainland by passenger-only Stewart Island Experience, while the main Hauraki Gulf Islands are served by Fullers ferries or Sealink out of Auckland.

Time

New Zealand follows UTC/GMT +12, with daylight saving putting clocks one hour ahead between October and March, when it becomes UTC/GMT+13.

Tipping

Until recently tipping was not a New Zealand custom, but the practice is gradually spreading, at least in towns. It's not necessary to leave a tip, therefore, though you might want to round up the bill or perhaps add on a gratuity of around 5 per cent if you feel the service has been exceptional.

Water

Tap water is safe to drink though might have a chlorinated taste, and is served free in restaurants. Be careful with running spring water out in the countryside—no matter how clean it looks, it's hard to be sure that the water has not been contaminated by bugs.

General editor
Barbara Ender-Jones

Updating
Julia Schoon
Claude Hervé-Bazin

Design
Karin Palazzolo

Layout
Luc Malherbe

Photo credits
P. 1: Corbis/McKee
P. 2: istockphoto.com/Bartlett
(fern); Corbis/Souders (kiwi sign);
Guy Minder (whale);
Bruce King (carving)

Maps
JPM Publications,
Mathieu Germay

Copyright © 2012, 2007
by JPM Publications S.A.
12, avenue William-Fraisse,
1006 Lausanne, Switzerland
information@jpmguides.com
http://www.jpmguides.com/

Printed in Switzerland
13639.00.13191
Edition 2012–2013